# THE KILLER WITHIN

# THE KILLER

# WITHIN

## An African Look at Disease, Sin and Keeping Yourself Saved

Mike Taliaferro

DPI
DISCIPLESHIP
PUBLICATIONS
INTERNATIONAL

**The Killer Within**

©1997 by Discipleship Publications International
2 Sterling Road, Billerica, MA 01862-2595

Printed in the United States of America

Book layout and design by Chris Costello
Cover Images ©1997 PhotoDisc, Inc.

ISBN 1-57782-042-8

To Anne-Brigitte—
words cannot describe
my love and admiration

# CONTENTS

# Of Locked Doors, Vampires and Guinea Worms

When Jesus said that he would build a church and the gates of Hell would not prevail against it, he didn't just mean that the kingdom corporate was indestructible. Peter's individual confession "You are the Christ" pioneered the way for millions of such confessions to follow, confessions that can start a soul journey that leads to eternal life. And that makes the individual capable, through Jesus Christ, to be impervious to the assaults of Hell, as well.

For years we have said that the church cannot be hurt from outside attacks nearly as much as inside attacks, usually meaning that no one can do more damage to the cause than the disgruntled member or the false brother. But the real inside attacks come long before a person's heart is swayed to hurt the church. We can be prepared to repel those attacks, because Jesus said the kingdom is within us. And he said the gates of Hell cannot prevail against the kingdom. The gates of Hell cannot prevail against the individual disciple of Jesus, unless that individual disciple *allows* the enemy to come inside.

Mike Taliaferro has been both witness to and a target of suffering. Diagnosed with cancer three years ago, Mike endured the radiation treatments that ultimately allowed the doctors to pronounce him cured. But his courage in the face of death revealed a strength that came from knowing that an enemy wasn't just attacking the inside of his body. The devil was also striking deep inside God's territory, the domain of his Christian heart. Thank God that the gates of Hell did not prevail against Mike Taliaferro.

This little book is timely. With so many leaders in churches around the world concerned about what attacks the devil is planning from the outside—negative articles about the church on the Internet, in the newspapers, on the television, on the campuses and in the offices—we all need to be reminded that the church is impervious to attacks from the outside. In fact, the bastions of Hell can not prevent us from going in and dragging lost souls out of the flames to salvation.

Such universal corporate power of the church is demonstrated daily on what many consider a mundane, commonplace playing field: the everyday life of the everyday disciple of Jesus. That life can be indestructible; that life can be eternally glorious.

For twelve years I lived in Manhattan, and now for three years I've lived in a northern suburb of the city. One thing I've noticed folks do in both places: They lock their doors at night. Some people lock their doors all the time and still worry that a bad guy will get in. They take all kinds of security measures and often get a dog that will bite, if not a gun that will shoot. This book isn't really about physical sickness, though Mike's got some stuff in here that made me pucker my face and spin away from the pages several times. (The Guinea worms are my gnarliest nightmare.) This book uses cholera, cancer and creepy, scary, real monsters to allegorize an equally frightening and real threat to our well-being—the evil that Satan tries to get us to entertain on the inside, an evil that, like the legend of Dracula, cannot come in unless invited and will not go away without drastic measures being taken.

So, grab a hammer and a stake. Start reading this book. Lock out all the monsters that want to get into your heart, because we all need your heart to be unprevailed against. You *are* the kingdom.

*Steve Johnson*
*New York City*

# Come with Me
# to Africa

*Jesus said to them, "It is not the healthy
who need a doctor, but the sick. I have not come
to call the righteous, but sinners"*

Mark 2:17

# AFRICA

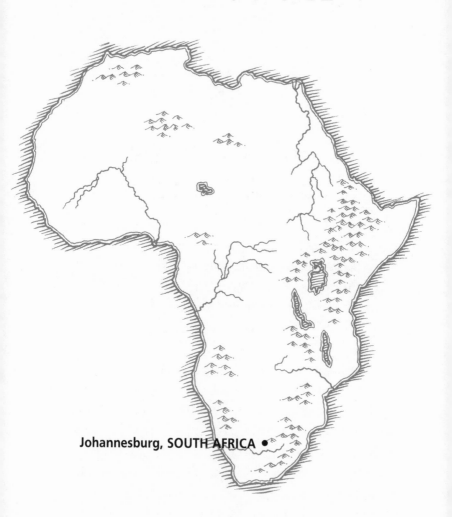

Johannesburg, SOUTH AFRICA ●

$\mathbf{I}$n Jesus' own eyes his primary mission on this planet was to save souls and restore mankind's relationship with God. He came as the Great Physician, seeing clearly the need all of us have for redemption. His love drove him to take on human form with all of its trials and tribulations and to live a life that would serve as both the perfect example and the perfect sacrifice on the cross at Calvary.

To this divine physician, the problem facing all people is sin. Sin is the plague that haunts mankind. It not only destroys the beautiful life God intended for us, but it also robs us of our eternal relationship with the Creator. Jesus called himself the doctor, and sin is the disease he treats.

Today many people in the developed world have forgotten the horrors of disease. Clinics, hospitals, vaccinations and modern treatments have given many the chance to live much longer lives than even just a century ago. Many are insured, removing also the fear of the exorbitant cost of treatment. Diseases such as smallpox and polio are a distant memory. Illnesses like the plague and tetanus are thought to be extinct, with the tetanus shot a mere formality. In some ways the power of Jesus' medical analogy is lost on those living under the blanket of "modern medicine." The horror of disease has been forgotten.

Africans, however, have not forgotten. Although the health care today is far ahead of what Africans received just fifty years ago, disease is still a formidable enemy to the modern African fighting for his family's survival.

My prayer is that this book will help you to know a little more about Africa and the wonderful people who live here. I also hope that you will grow in your respect for the people who struggle daily to exist in what is often a very harsh environment. Most of all, I hope to awaken you to the horrors of disease which Jesus himself faced in the first century. When Jesus called sin a disease, it evoked a powerful picture in the minds of his hearers. It is this picture which I present to you here. Hopefully, by under-standing sin a little better, we will all grow in our conviction that sin *must* be quickly repented of and avoided. Prayerfully, these convictions will enable you to stay free from sin's tyranny and remain faithful for a lifetime.

*Mike Taliaferro*
*Johannesburg, 1997*

# CHAPTER 1

# Ebola

*"I will bring upon you sudden terror,
wasting diseases and fever that
will destroy your sight and drain away your life."*

Leviticus 26:16

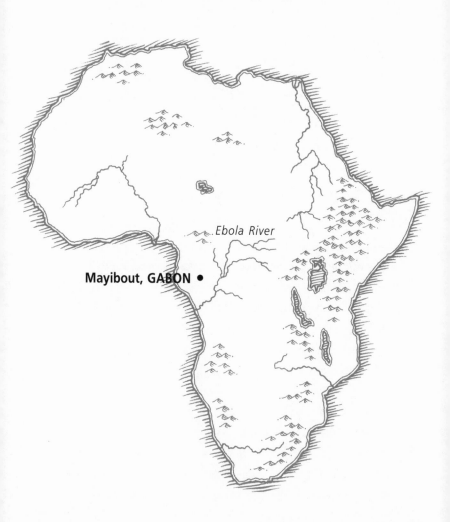

# AFRICA

*Ebola River*

**Mayibout, GABON** •

Mayibout village lies just north of the equator in the jungles of the central African nation of Gabon. The residents of Mayibout, a tiny village set back in the trees near the Ivindo River, live in one of the most beautiful regions of central Africa. Rain forests, mountains, rivers, waterfalls and abundant wildlife make it appear almost like paradise.

Mayibout's location is remote. Take the nine-hour canoe trip to the provincial capital of Makokou, and you would find an airport, along with tarred roads. Makokou has about twelve thousand inhabitants, some hotels and a nightclub. There are also telephones there that might be working.

The canoe trip up from Makokou to Mayibout is stunning. Green hills roll on, seemingly forever. Wildlife is so abundant that the Worldwide Fund for Nature has initiated efforts to turn the area into a protected reserve. Great numbers of elephants still roam the lush jungles. They soak themselves by day in the river to keep cool, and you can hear them crashing through the forest at night, eating leaves and scratching themselves against the trees. Some lowland gorillas still survive. Occasionally, a family of gorillas can be spotted high up in the fruit trees. Birdlife is everywhere, and at night great flocks of parrots actively entertain the villagers along the river. Monkeys race through the treetops constantly, chattering and screeching in an endless whirlwind of activity.

Mayibout village itself is not so impressive. There is no telephone service and no electricity. The buildings are like concrete boxes with corrugated tin roofs. Most residents live in mud huts with thatch overhead. It is hot. There's a lot of malaria in the village, and health care is minimal.

Thomas and Jacques lived in Mayibout. Their families were neighbors who farmed small plots outside the village. One morning in February 1996 the two boys woke up early to go and work in their parents' fields. Walking out together, they played as usual on their way to do their chores. That morning, however, was different. They noticed in the undergrowth nearby what appeared to be a dead animal. Approaching slowly, they saw that it was a large chimpanzee lying lifeless in the tall grass. They stood still for several seconds to see if it was breathing. Then the two boys grabbed the chimpanzee by the arms and pulled it into the pathway.

The children were absolutely delighted! "Bush meat" is a delicacy in the rain forests of eastern Gabon. Small antelope, porcupine or even some rodents are eaten, but chimpanzees are especially appreciated for their size and flavor. They knew their families would be excited about their discovery. They tried to drag the chimpanzee down the pathway, but they found him too heavy. Leaving him in the path, they raced off to find help to carry the dead animal home, unaware that every ounce of flesh in the chimpanzee was saturated with perhaps the most deadly virus on the planet.

Several villagers came out to help the boys bring the dead primate home. They carried the animal to a neighbor's home, where they laid him out on an old wooden table. A villager brought out a knife and began to skin the chimp.

Undoubtedly, a fire was quickly started. Soon chunks of meat were being sliced off and thrown over the flames. At this point the virus had several possible entry points into its new human hosts. While butchering the animal, perhaps a bloody hand passed over a small cut on the villager's arm. Perhaps fluids were splattered into the eyes or mouth. Perhaps some undercooked meat was eaten. The specifics of the transmission may never be known, but Mayibout village was about to come face to face with dreaded Ebola, a disease that kills approximately eighty-five percent of those infected. Without knowing it, at least a dozen people were infected with the organism. The cookout continued all afternoon, but the virus immediately got to work.

After the chimpanzee cookout in Mayibout village, everyone went home to sleep. The little Ebola virus, however, does not sleep. Although it is so small that over one hundred million could fit on the period at the end of this sentence, it multiplies so quickly that your body is transformed into a virtual virus bag within days, with every cell in your body affected. Indeed, sometimes the virus multiplies so quickly that the cells can literally pop open.

One of those who skinned the chimp that day in Mayibout soon began to feel the symptoms. First comes the headache. Within seven days of infection comes a throbbing pain behind the eyes. Next comes the backache, followed by vomiting and a high fever. The victim's face sets itself into an expressionless stare. The eyeballs become bright red. The victim's demeanor turns ugly—there is anger, resentment and antagonism. Within the bloodstream, Ebola attacks relentlessly. As it destroys body cells, the blood begins to coagulate at a furious pace. Blood clots form, thickening and slowing the blood. These clots cause vital tissue to die in the liver, kidneys, stomach and brain. Ebola attacks connective tissues with particular ferocity. The face sags, organs dissolve and a victim might even slough off the skin of the tongue as he pours out a disgusting black vomit mixed with blood. Soon the blood loses the ability to coagulate and the victim begins to bleed from every opening in his body.

No one knows where Ebola lives in the wild. Somewhere in the forests of central Africa is an animal or insect which can carry the virus without being harmed. Chimpanzees and mon-keys die as quickly as humans do once infected. Scientists from various organizations have scoured the jungles looking for the pathogen's host, but so far they have had no success. It could be a spider, a bat or some type of rodent. No one knows.

What we do know is that Ebola brings on a gruesome and terrifying death. In 1976 some nuns running a hospital in what was then northern Zaire (today called the Republic of Congo) treated a man who wandered in with a high fever. They gave him an injection and then re-used the syringe on many other patients during the day. Within days the virus erupted in fifty-five villages near the hospital. First, it killed the people who had received the contaminated injections. Next, it attacked family members—especially women, who in Zaire prepare the dead for burial. Finally, it wiped out most of the nursing staff at the hos-pital. President Mobutu of Zaire called in the army to quarantine the hospital and the local chiefs were already closing off their villages to travelers. Because the hospital was situated near the Ebola river, the name "Ebola Virus" stuck. The virus burned itself out within about a month, leaving at least two hundred dead.

Ebola, in its present form, could not destroy the human population. Because it kills its host within a few days, it doesn't have enough time to widely infect a large number of people. Unlike influenza, which can be spread through the air, Ebola is spread through body fluids (blood, saliva, vomit, semen, etc.). Ebola strikes fear into people's hearts not because of the large numbers who die, but because of the gruesome manner in which they die.

Death can occur as a result of a dozen different causes. Perhaps a key organ will fail, or the victim will simply bleed to death. Oftentimes seizures signal the final moments as the brain begins to die off, piece by piece. By the time someone dies there are already sections of his flesh decomposing.

At least fifteen people died of Ebola in Mayibout village as a result of the bush-meat cookout. The Gabonese government quickly quarantined the area and contained the damage. Within days scientists from the World Health Organization were making the canoe trip from Makokou to Mayibout. Somewhere out in that beautiful forest, in the bloodstream of some animal or insect, lurks a terrible killer. Scientists still do not know where it is hiding, but they do know it will surface again among humans. And, as every villager in Mayibout knows, Ebola does not give its victims a second chance.

✝

We live in a world which is wide awake to the dangers of physical illness. Ebola terrifies people who are exposed to it. We avoid countries where outbreaks are reported. Others flee villages where the virus is found. We cringe at reports of people dissolving and bleeding to death within an eight-day period. We applaud the strong measures taken to protect the populace: the army called in, villages sealed off, experts flown in, etc.

Ebola is approached in a way similar to the AIDS virus. Billions of dollars are spent researching AIDS. Fear of the virus has caused millions to change their sexual practices. Organizations work endlessly to educate the public. All of this is good and is needed, and we applaud all these efforts.

Yet, another epidemic rages throughout our world today almost completely unnoticed. Far more deadly than Ebola, or even AIDS, this epidemic is wrecking families and destroying lives around the world. Millions stand in need of education. Nations need to be warned. Lives need to be saved. As shocking as it may seem, some who are aware of this epidemic are still lackluster in their responses. They stand exposed and unprotected against the greatest killer of all time. That killer is sin.

Disregard for the standards of God, attitudes and behavior contrary to the will of God, living by our own desires and not by God's plan—all this is sin. The epidemic of sin has engulfed our world in an appalling way. Millions believe that immorality is normal and to be expected. Drunkenness is acceptable. Divorce is common. In some American cities today, there are actually more abortions than births. Racism, and ethnic and tribal hatred still live in the hearts and minds of millions. In the "enlightened" twentieth century, the number of people who have died in genocidal efforts is astounding.

In his book *The Empty Church*, Thomas C. Reeves writes this about the United States:

> Between 1960 and 1990, when the population increased 41 percent, there was a 560 percent increase in violent crime, a more than 400 percent increase in illegitimate births, a more than 200 percent rise in the teenage suicide rate, and a nearly 200 percent rise in divorce. The percentage of children living in single-parent homes had more than tripled during that period, and the fastest-growing segment of the criminal population was the nation's children.

> As of June 30, 1994, there were more than a million people in American prisons for the first time in history. The number was more than double that of 1984, and the ratio of prison population to the general public during that period had doubled.... *The Wall Street Journal*, pointed out that in 1991, 1.2 million children were born to unmarried mothers—practically 30 percent of all live births.

> Data released by the US Census Bureau in August 1994 showed that only 50.8 percent of American children lived in a traditional nuclear family (defined as one in which both biological parents were present and all children were born after the marriage). One-half of all African-American children, nearly one-third of Latino children, and one-fifth of white children lived with a single parent. According to one study, some 60 percent of the

nation's rapists, 72 percent of adolescent murderers, and 70 percent of long-term prisoners came from homes where the father was absent.*

Sin is the problem in America. The empty churches go hand in hand with the crowded jails. Absent fathers and easy divorce go hand in hand with illegitimate babies and abortions. The sin epidemic is running rampant, causing an inestimable amount of suffering in the lives of those affected.

The developing world faces similar struggles, of course. The rural towns and villages are emptying as Africans head for the cities. The traditions of the past are quickly giving way to the fast life of the urban centers. Sin is more rampant than disease in Africa.

Before, however, we become overly indignant about the world we live in, I would also like to ask you to look at yourself personally. In Mark 2:17 Jesus compares sin to disease and himself to the doctor:

> On hearing this, Jesus said to them, "It is not the healthy who need a doctor, but the sick. I have not come to call the righteous, but sinners."

He was talking about you and me. Paul writes in Romans 3:23 that "all have sinned and fall short of the glory of God." We all have the disease. Jesus says in Luke 13:3, "Unless you repent,

*Thomas C. Reeves, *The Empty Church* (New York, NY: Free Press, 1996), 6-7.

you too will all perish." Sin is a killer to which we have all been exposed. We must take action, or else we will perish. This is no joke. It is reality.

One day in the Johannesburg city center, we were handing out information brochures about AIDS. The need is incredible: Of the general population aged fifteen to forty-five years old, at least fifteen percent now carry the HIV virus. In some African cities the infection rates approach forty percent. Yes, forty percent! One man, as he sauntered down the pavement, scoffed at the brochure. "AIDS," he said. "Ha! AIDS stands for American Invention to Destroy Sex. There's no AIDS!" At best the man is sadly misinformed. At worst he is a fool who will soon lie infected in a city hospital. In this day and age if you do not take the virus seriously, it will probably kill you.

I see the same attitude toward sin in many people. I share my faith with people who scoff at the dangers of sin. They believe in Jesus, but they do not take seriously his warnings about sin, ruined lives and hell.

I speak with disciples of Jesus who say they are struggling with sin. Whatever the costs, they would flee an Ebola outbreak if they were near it, yet they cannot seem to take seriously the spiritual disease which will harm them from now through eternity.

Some feel like giving up. Others have lost the fight they once had. They have allowed the virus of sin to creep into their hearts. That is what this book is all about: staying in the fight and winning it, maintaining your spiritual health, and recapturing the conviction to say no to sin. Your very survival depends on it.

Victory over sin begins with a healthy respect for the spiritual virus which attacks you. We all respect Ebola. Men and women in the biohazard units of the military wear something akin to space suits when handling it. You cannot help but respect a microscopic virus which can transform your body within a few days into a sack of dissolving flesh.

Sin, however, deserves far more respect. As much suffering as Ebola would cause you, sin causes more. Again, Jesus says, "I tell you, no! But unless you repent, you too will all perish." You cannot go to heaven living a sinful life. We will repent, or else we will perish. The writer of Hebrews teaches us:

> If we deliberately keep on sinning after we have received the knowledge of the truth, no sacrifice for sins is left, but only a fearful expectation of judgment and of raging fire that will consume the enemies of God (10:26-27).

So many denominational preachers today stress God's love, mercy and patience. This is all well and good. Still, in order to understand God's love, we must understand God's justice. Sin will be punished. Hell is real. The suffering which Ebola causes pales in comparison to the horrible pain of hell. If God's love will not motivate you, perhaps God's judgment will. We must wake up. Sin is not the common cold. It is a killer disease which we must take seriously.

Sin causes suffering, and this is not limited to hell. Like any illness, sin makes you miserable right here on earth. For example, read Galatians 5:19-21 carefully:

> The acts of the sinful nature are obvious: sexual immorality, impurity and debauchery; idolatry and witchcraft; hatred, discord, jealousy, fits of rage, selfish ambition, dissensions, factions and envy; drunkenness, orgies, and the like. I warn you, as I did before, that those who live like this will not inherit the kingdom of God.

Just as Ebola affects you emotionally, so does sin. Sin directly attacks and contaminates your emotional well-being. Consider anger. Who would say his temper has enriched his life? Those with a hot temper suffer the loneliness of lost friends and broken marriages, along with the guilt of inflicting so much pain.

What about sexual immorality? Was the momentary pleasure worth it? The young cannot seem to understand why God limits sex to married couples. But God's wisdom becomes clearer once they have contracted syphilis or gonorrhea. God's wisdom is obvious to one who has contracted AIDS from a prostitute. Let's be honest. Deep down, don't you regret that abortion? Didn't you feel used at times when your "lover" only wanted physical gratification and then simply discarded you like a rented video?

One of the most horrible moments in my life came in 1978. My roommate had a girlfriend who kept asking me to go out with her secretly. I refused. Finally, she asked me to dinner right in front of her boyfriend, my roommate. She made it seem so harmless that even my roommate encouraged me to go. I accepted the invitation, and we went out together. It was an incredible mistake. Coming home from dinner, we parked the car in a deserted spot. Although we did not sleep together, there was much impurity. The next day I went to class as usual.

About three weeks later my roommate confronted me about what had happened, and almost twenty years later I can still see the look on his face that day. His girlfriend had confessed, and I felt sick to my stomach because there was absolutely no place to hide. I can only imagine how betrayed he felt. It was one stupid moment of pleasure which I have regretted for years. You can only imagine how uncomfortable it was living with him for the rest of the semester. Sin ruins relationships.

Another horrible memory is of a good friend going to the doctor as a teenager to get a blood test. He suspected that he had a sexually transmitted disease. The results were negative, but he felt so stupid. There he was, face to face with his family doctor who had known his parents for all those years. He wished that he could crawl under a rock to hide. Today, it always reminds me that sin might bring pleasure in the short term, but godly living brings pleasure in the long term.

Sin makes you miserable. Never have I heard someone say, "Lying has brought meaning to my life," or " My envy and jealousy have been so enjoyable." Rather, sin brings guilt, regret and disappointment. Like Ebola, it destroys your future. And like Ebola, it destroys your present as well.

All those villagers in Gabon who ate the chimpanzee enjoyed the meal. The cooked flesh brought pleasure as they feasted that day. Later on, you can imagine the regret they felt as their bodies melted from within and as they were transformed into walking zombies whose major organs were literally being dissolved.

A call went out by the Gabonese government warning villagers about the dangers of bush meat. The call was heeded, and the outbreak subsided. But oh, how we need to heed the warning today! Don't be duped into the suffering of hell simply to enjoy a few fleeting moments of pleasure. To eat the infected chimpanzee was truly tragic. To eat it after being warned would be simply idiotic.

Ebola is a molecular shark—a biological killer. Sin is also a killer. Sin will surely break you down, wring all the joy from your life and annihilate you spiritually. It destroys your future; it dissolves your relationships; and it sends you to hell. Consider yourself warned.

But stay with me. We are going to find some solutions. Jesus is the Great Physician, and you can set up an appointment with him today!

# CHAPTER 2

# Cholera

*...and sin, when it is full-grown,
gives birth to death.*

James 1:15

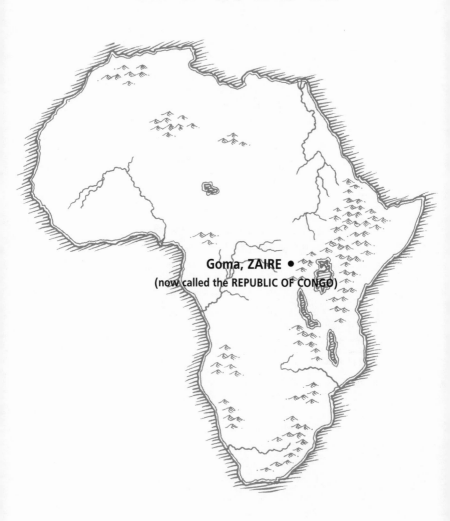

# AFRICA

**Goma, ZAIRE** ●
(now called the REPUBLIC OF CONGO)

The scene simply defied the imagination. On Thursday, July 14, 1994, the Zairians threw open the border gates and allowed the fleeing Rwandans to cross the border. The Hutu people from all over Rwanda streamed across the border like a human tidal wave. The town of Goma, Zaire (now called the Republic of Congo), doubled in size in one day. Ragged refugees flooded past the check point at a rate of ten thousand people per hour. The mass exodus caught relief workers unprepared for the medical emergency which soon developed. Literally, within a few days almost two million Rwandans fled their country, spilling across into Zaire and Tanzania. Eight hundred thousand came to Goma alone. There was little shelter or drinkable water to be found. It was everyone's worst nightmare. But it would get worse.

Cholera struck the camps. Within ten days the United Nations was describing the cholera epidemic as "out of control."

Up to three thousand people were dying daily. It was hell on earth. How did all of this happen?

Pygmies have always lived in Rwanda as far back as anyone can tell. Because there is no written history of Rwanda before the 1800s, no one can say exactly when the other two tribes arrived. The Hutu people came in about 1000 A.D. The Tutsis apparently arrived in 1600. Over the last four hundred years the Tutsis have dominated the Hutus, cultivating a lord-peasant relationship in a feudal system of land ownership.

When the Belgians colonized Rwanda in 1916, they favored the Tutsis by administrating the country through them. The Tutsis received all the advantages in the army, education and government employment. Exacerbating the situation was the fact that eighty-five percent of the population was Hutu. Only fourteen percent were Tutsi.

By the time independence came in 1962, Belgium had a change of heart. Their sympathies now ran with the majority Hutus, whom they left in power after their departure. For the next three decades the Tutsis were the oppressed people. Many crossed the border into Zaire and Uganda to train for a military overthrow and return to power in Rwanda.

Eventually, the French put pressure on the Hutu government to bring home the Tutsis who had fled, as well as to stop persecuting the Tutsis within Rwanda. The Hutu president, Juvenal Habyarimana, was also being pressured by Hutu extremists who felt that extermination of the Tutsis was the only way to secure their position. Indeed, the Hutus had a command structure in place to facilitate the planned genocide.

The turning point came on April 6, 1994. The president, returning home from a peace conference in Tanzania, was killed when rocket fire shot down and destroyed his airplane.

The attacker's identity is still a mystery, but before the president's death had been publicly announced, death lists were being circulated in the capital. Cell groups had been organized, and Tutsis were all targeted for genocide.

Road blocks were thrown up everywhere. If the name on your identity card was a Tutsi name, you were murdered on the spot. Neighbors killed neighbors; teachers killed pupils. Shop owners were killed by their customers. Tutsis fled to stadiums and churches seeking protection, but to no avail. The churches were the scenes of some of the worst massacres. Six thousand died in one Cyahinda church alone. It was utter madness.

As Tutsis fled into hiding in the jungles, the world simply turned a blind eye. General Romeo Dallaire, who had learned of the plot in advance, was commander of the UN forces in Rwanda. He begged the UN for reinforcements. Instead, his forces were cut to only 270 troops. Later he said that with only 5,000 troops he could have saved 500,000 lives.

So many Tutsis were killed that their dead bodies clogged the river Nyaborongo on its way to Lake Victoria. The Hutu radio joked about it being the shortest way out for the Tutsis. In the end, as many as 750,000 Tutsis were murdered.

Within days of the genocide's beginning, there was a dramatic turn of events. Tutsi militias in Uganda crossed the border into Rwanda to rescue their people and retake the country. In a series of brilliant maneuvers, the disciplined Tutsis chased the Hutu army across the border into Zaire. Along with the army went refugees as well, fleeing certain retribution by the Tutsis. The two million Hutu refugees streamed into Zaire like the Israelites out of the Red Sea. Because there was no sanitation, little drinkable water and very little medical care, cholera broke out with a fury.

Cholera is caused by a bacterial infection of the intestinal lining. Initial symptoms are abdominal pains and diarrhea, which, in extreme cases, can be excreted almost continuously. Although there is no fever, the sufferer becomes extremely thirsty. Cholera causes its victim to pass up to fifteen liters (four gallons) of fluid a day. Obviously, this kind of dehydration can quickly lead to death, which is exactly what happened in Zaire. The refugees died by the thousands.

I sat on the balcony of the Hotel Residence in Bukavu, Zaire, in September of 1994. Bukavu had been inundated with 400,000 refugees, and we had gone there to ascertain whether HOPE Worldwide could do something for Rwanda. After a day of touring the camps and speaking to UN officials, I spoke with a nurse from a Scottish aid organization about the cholera outbreak.

"They came across the border at a rate of 600 per minute," she began. "Many had cholera before they arrived. Some stumbled into town. Others had to be helped. We stuck IVs into their arms as quickly as we could, but you could see that they were dying faster than we could help them."

"It was truly pathetic. The volcanic soil was so hard that we couldn't dig any latrines. We had to scrape together some top-soil and situate the latrines atop mounds of dirt. Some were so weak that they couldn't even crawl up the short slope to the door. Later the French dug mass graves the size of soccer fields. Still, they overflowed."

Eventually, the epidemic burned itself out, but not before 50,000 people had died.[*]

☩

Cholera can be easily prevented by drinking pure water and eating only clean vegetables. If you drink contaminated water, however, you will eventually contract the disease. It's inevitable, and the vaccine is not very effective. It lasts only a short time. Physically speaking, you must be very careful about what you pump into your system. If you insist on ingesting contaminated fluids, you will fall sick sooner or later.

The same is true spiritually. Christians must be concerned about purity. Just like the poor Rwandan refugees who, out of necessity, drank the contaminated waters around them and died, I see Christians today who are weak and feeble because they are

[*]As I edit this in 1997, most of the refugees have now returned to Rwanda.

constantly "drinking in" spiritual impurities. I speak with people who are thinking of becoming Christians yet cannot muster the strength to make the slightest progress toward God. Their systems are full of the impurities which they can't seem to give up.

The apostle Paul put it this way in 1 Thessalonians 4:3-8:

> *It is God's will that you should be sanctified: that you should avoid sexual immorality; that each of you should learn to control his own body in a way that is holy and honorable, not in passionate lust like the heathen, who do not know God; and that in this matter no one should wrong his brother or take advantage of him. The Lord will punish men for all such sins, as we have already told you and warned you. For God did not call us to be impure, but to live a holy life. Therefore, he who rejects this instruction does not reject man but God, who gives you his Holy Spirit.*

God feels strongly about Christians keeping impurities out of our lives. Indeed, he says that if we reject this instruction then we have rejected God himself.

Spiritual impurities come at us today from all directions. Besides the obvious prostitute who walks the pavements of most major cities, impurity creeps into our lives from a variety of sources. Family video stores stock pornography; cybersex is only a click or two away on the Internet; bookstores have pornographic magazines; movies inevitably have a sexual scene between unmarried lovers; music lyrics blatantly romanticize impurity; advertisers use lust and sex to sell their products; and flirtatious coworkers are often ready to hop into bed. Impurity is everywhere. It surrounds, bombards and entices throughout the day. To say that sensual bombardment has no impact on the modern Christian is obviously absurd.

But God is concerned not just with our maintaining our purity in our actions, but in our thoughts as well. Matthew 5:27-28 spells it out clearly for the disciple:

> *"You have heard that it was said, 'Do not commit adultery.' But I tell you that anyone who looks at a woman lustfully has already committed adultery with her in his heart."*

Looking lustfully is a sin. But Jesus goes further:

> *"If your right eye causes you to sin, gouge it out and throw it away. It is better for you to lose one part of your body than for your whole body to be thrown into hell" (Matthew 5:29).*

You cannot call yourself a Christian if you dive headlong into lust. Indeed, lust leads you to hell. Jesus' point is both clear and empathetic: Stand up and decide today that you will stop lusting. David says it this way: "I will set before my eyes no vile thing" (Psalm 101:3).

Brothers, have you sneaked a look at some pornographic magazine at the store? Do you rent pornographic videos? Have you gone into a peep show or massage parlor? Do you search for adult entertainment on the Internet? Sisters, have you "escaped" into romance novels filled with lusty scenes and illicit sex? Do you buy the tabloid-type magazines that describe the affairs of the rich and famous? Do you catch the soap operas when you don't have work? (My friends in the States tell me that pretty much all soap operas have gotten lustful and trashy.)

These aren't just mistakes. These are sinful decisions that will kill you spiritually. Committing these sins is like inviting spiritual cholera to flow through your veins. Soon you will have no strength left whatsoever. After filling your system with impurities, you become like the Rwandan refugee who cannot muster the strength to crawl up the small mound to the latrine.

How sad it is when someone is so infected with sin that now he "can't" read his Bible, "struggles" to come to church services and is just "too weak" to say no to temptations. How did she arrive at such a pathetic situation, saying things like, "I want to change, but I can't"? The answer is simple. When he insists on contaminating his system with impurity, he will get sick and eventually die.

Cholera works quickly. You can go from good health to a pine coffin within a few days. Such is the power of the bacteria. I see something very similar in the spiritual world. I see young, vibrant Christians who are genuinely excited for God, love to read their Bibles, are eager to pray and are excited to share their faith. But then they allow Satan to pollute their hearts with impurities, and a change takes place. The impurity begins to affect them. Soon they are turning into weak disciples who cannot even manage a short prayer in the morning. Evangelism becomes difficult. Church services become a burden.

Watch out for impurity! It steals your strength. It robs you of conviction. It transforms you into a spiritual weakling. More than once, promising disciples have been eaten alive by this spiritual cholera. The impurities they allowed into their hearts quickly drained away the conviction and joy of their discipleship, killing them spiritually.

✝

The truth is that if you are not careful about impurity, you will not survive for long as a disciple. It's that simple. At one time I led a Bible discussion group and was assisted by a seemingly strong disciple. He had a responsible job, a beautiful family and a promising future. We had a blast together, evangelizing and studying the Bible with many people who became Christians. He seemed in great spiritual health, as solid as a rock.

In situations like this, Satan is no fool. He knows that you will not fall for the big, obvious temptations. Instead he begins chipping away at your convictions. Piece by piece he erodes your footing and your foundation.

My friend, he lowered his guard in a few areas. Ignoring pornography turned into glancing at pornography, which soon turned into buying it regularly. He went for massages. He flirted with coworkers. Satan's plan took time to hatch, but the end of the story is that he left God, left his wife and children and moved in with a coworker. Spiritual cholera had cut him down.

We must strive for purity in all areas because sloppiness can destroy us. Impurity is a real and deadly enemy. Starting small, impurity will not remain stagnant in your life. It seeks to grow and dominate you. Too many disciples have become weakened and have fallen because they did not say no to sin. Too many disciples have suffered spiritually because they said that this "one small sin" won't matter. But it does matter—don't let down your guard!

Once on the road in Kenya, I pulled into a roadside store for a snack. Normally I don't eat road food in Africa because of the lack of refrigeration and freshness. But I was hungry, and a meat pie looked too good to resist. *Just this once,* I thought to myself. *Surely this one little meat pie won't kill me.* It almost did. I woke up that night in my bed with the worst case of food poisoning I can remember. I vomited so loudly that my wife woke up thinking that there was an animal dying outside the window.

I learned a great lesson: I would not allow a temptation to entice me "just this once." Don't let Satan lead you by the nose toward destruction. The cholera bacteria is so small that, although you need a microscope to see it, it still wreaks havoc in your life.

Impurity is exactly the same. Although it is seemingly small, it is equally deadly.

✠

In all this danger, however, there lurks some hope. Cholera is easy to cure if you act quickly. You can return to full health with no long term effects if you rapidly replace the body fluids you are losing with clean water. There was no clean water for the Rwandans, and there was no wood to use for building a fire to boil the water. The refugees were helpless.

We, on the other hand, are not helpless before impurity. We can move quickly to replace the fluids and restore the strength that we've lost, if we act decisively. You don't have to be a push-over for sin. You don't have to be a pathetic wimp. You can decide your spiritual destiny.

For the prevention and the cure, *first, dive into God's word to rejuvenate your faith.* Psalm 119:9-11 tells us that if we will spend time in God's word we can keep our way pure:

*How can a young man keep his way pure?*
*By living according to your word.*
*I seek you with all my heart;*
*do not let me stray from your commands.*
*I have hidden your word in my heart*
*that I might not sin against you (Psalm 119:9-11).*

God's word is like spiritual Gatorade. You will be amazed at how regular Bible study will amplify and reinforce your convictions about sin. Do you want to get well? Do you want to stay well? Then start reading your Bible, and read it day after day after day!

*Second, avoid the bookstores, the video stores, the tabloids and the television programs where the impurity is found.* Break off the immoral relationships that are dragging you down. Change any pattern in your dating relationship that is tempting you to sin. As you read these scriptures below, feel the passion of the Holy Spirit about avoiding sexual sin:

> *Flee from sexual immorality. All other sins a man commits are outside his body, but he who sins sexually sins against his own body (1 Corinthians 6:18).*

> *Flee the evil desires of youth, and pursue righteousness, faith, love and peace, along with those who call on the Lord out of a pure heart (2 Timothy 2:22).*

*Third, find a close friend you can talk to about your struggles.* Don't try to fight this battle alone. All of us have battled with impurity, and we can help each other if we will be open. (Of course, sometimes it's not just the impurity which we must avoid. Sometimes it's the situations that *lead* to impurity which we must avoid, as well.)

One area where some wisdom is required is in dating relationships. Obviously, the Bible teaches that sex is reserved for marriage. God is not anti-sex; nor is God anti-fun. Rather, God has designed the marriage relationship as the proper environment for sexual relations. This nurturing atmosphere of commitment and love is the proper place for physical relations. I do not apologize for this belief, regardless of how old-fashioned it may sound to some. The truth is that after seeing all the abortions, the sexually transmitted diseases and the single-parent families which the sexual revolution has spawned, God's plan looks wiser and wiser with every passing year.

Regarding dating, however, sometimes I hear the question, "Show me the scripture which says I can't sit alone in my house with my girlfriend." The obvious answer is that there is no scripture forbidding it. Only impurity is forbidden. Judging whether a situation will lead to impurity is up to the individual Christian.

However, I do give this advice: Date without being dumb. There are no scriptures which say you cannot play football on the freeway. There is no scripture that says you cannot get out of your car and pet lions in the game park. It is not forbidden; it is simply stupid.

In the same way, beware of being alone with your date in a car parked in a remote place on a dark, moonlit Saturday night. If you play with fire, you are going to get burned. Don't be naive!

✠

Several years ago I took a class on CPR (Cardio-Pulmonary Resuscitation). The instructor told us about a time when he was trying to resuscitate an older man who had had a heart attack and had stopped breathing. As another man stood by and watched, my instructor worked hard to save the victim's life. He pumped on his chest to move the man's blood. Then he gave mouth-to-mouth resuscitation to push fresh air into his lungs. After several minutes the man was still not responding, nor was the ambulance arriving.

At this point the bystander told my instructor to give up. "It's no use," he said. "The man has already died."

The instructor still held on to a thread of hope that perhaps he could still revive the victim. Working hard for several more minutes, he began to tire physically. He also had to block out the negative comments which the bystander was making about how the victim was already dead.

Finally, the old man coughed. Then he began to breathe for himself. Then his pulse returned. Amazingly enough, by the time the ambulance arrived the man was actually conscious and alert.

The next day the instructor visited the old man in the hospital.

"Son," the man started, "I want to thank you for saving my life."

"It was nothing, really," he replied.

"Well," the man said, "I just wanted to let you know something."

"What's that?" the instructor asked, leaning in.

"Yesterday, when you were working on me, I could hear everything you and that other man were saying. I couldn't speak, but I could hear him telling you to give up because he thought I was dead."

"You heard all that?" the instructor asked, his eyes widening.

"I heard it all," the old man responded. "Thank you for staying with me like you did."

I know that some who are reading this book have been involved in sin for a long time. Perhaps your friends or loved ones are even starting to give up on you spiritually. When you do go to church services, you look like you are dead or dying spiritually. You don't show many signs of life or interest in Jesus. Perhaps some are thinking, "It's no use. He's a lost cause."

I don't agree. The fact that you are still reading this book shows that you are not a lost cause. The fact that you have read this far tells me that you are still alive. Indeed, I know you are listening. I know you can hear me.

You can revive yourself spiritually. It is not too late. You can recover fully in Jesus. There is still time. You can be like that old man who fought hard, hung on and lived through it all. I know there is still hope.

Those Rwandan refugees, when they crossed the border, were already beyond cure. As gallantly as the doctors and nurses labored on, the people still died by the thousands.

In our lives, however, it is different. We can open our Bibles, cut out the impurity and get help from one another. We can defeat the spiritual cholera which seeks to dehydrate us all. We can win the victory. I know you're listening. I know you can hear me.

# CHAPTER 3

# Cancer

*Is there no balm in Gilead?*
*Is there no physician there?*
*Why then is there no healing*
*for the wound of my people?*

Jeremiah 8:22

AFRICA

Mount Kilimanjaro ▲

Johannesburg, SOUTH AFRICA ●

As dawn broke on March 4, 1994, I stood atop Mount Kilimanjaro in Tanzania enjoying the 200-mile view across the east African savannah. It was breathtaking. I literally stood three miles above the villages and towns, and a full two miles above the clouds. At almost 20,000 feet above sea level, I felt I was on top of the world. Clouds stretched out before me like small puffs of cotton on a huge continental tabletop.

Several months of serious training had put me in top condition and had enabled me to reach the summit. My workouts had started with walking up the stairs of a sixteen-story apartment building. I progressed to running up. Eventually, I was running up *fourteen times* in one hour. That is the equivalent of running up the stairs of the Empire State Building *twice* in about fifty-five minutes!

As I stood atop Africa's tallest mountain, I felt like an "iron man." I was in great shape; I was still young at thirty-four years old, and I still clung tightly to the illusion that youth goes on forever, much like the Tanzanian plains of Africa. Death was something I never thought about. Old age was farther away than the nearest star, and my health was as sure as tomorrow's sunrise.

Then I started down the mountain...in more ways than one. Yes, I descended the three vertical miles to the plains below. But soon my health as well would be going downhill. Soon I would have my own brush with death. The iron man was about to become the trembling man of mere flesh.

The pains had begun during my training for Kilimanjaro. On one occasion I noticed severe pain in my lower abdomen after a stressful workout. In the next eighteen months, I had two or three other episodes of pain. I thought that it might be a hernia. All I could do then was lie down until the cramps passed. They always went away within twenty-four hours, but the pain was alarming. I spoke informally to doctors twice; each time they suggested that I had probably only pulled a muscle.

On November 9, 1995, I had another attack. I had worked out ferociously the day before and was lying in pain on the bed, unable to function. I knew I needed to go to a specialist and get some answers. Previously I had resisted this, but on that day I was urgent. The pain was simply too much. The urologist told me I could come in later that same day.

That Friday night I walked into Olivedale Clinic in Johannesburg, South Africa. I met the doctor at a reception area and followed him into an examination room. Twenty minutes later he looked at me and said the words we all dread hearing: "You have cancer."

The words hit me like a lightning bolt. I couldn't believe it. I simply stared at him, probably with my mouth wide open. He began to explain the details of my illness, but I wasn't listening. I had only heard the first three words. I sat on the bed with a blank look on my face.

Evidently I had a tumor attached to the left testicle which had enveloped the seminal tube. An operation would be needed, whether the tumor was malignant or benign. A biopsy was scheduled to confirm his diagnosis. Based on its location, however, the doctor was convinced that it was malignant (cancerous).

I understood that an operation would be necessary, but then the doctor said something to me that I will never forget: "How about tomorrow morning?"

Although I don't think I showed it on the outside, inside there was panic. I had never had surgery before, and yet right here before me was a doctor ready to cut me open in approximately fifteen hours. I would like to tell you that I took it like Rambo or Arnold. The truth is, I was terrified.

I was afraid of the surgery. I was afraid of the cancer. What if it had spread? What if I died? What about my wife and three children? This was all happening too quickly. Emotionally, I wanted to put this video on pause, step out of the situation and find some relief from the pressure. But life has no pause button. It was time to face the truth.

Agreeing to arrive at the hospital at 8:00 in the morning, I shook hands with my physician, and I walked out of the hospital to my car. I prayed all the way home.

The next three months were a blur of procedures, surgeries, tests and treatments. The initial operation was successful. The tumor was cancerous, but the doctor was optimistic about my prognosis. Next came a CAT-scan (a series of high-tech X-rays) to see if the cancer had spread. It revealed another tumor on my thyroid gland. Although the doctor felt this tumor was not cancerous, I was still frightened. I could only imagine the worst. A second operation was also a success. The second tumor was benign, and by early December the doctors were saying that things looked good and that they would monitor my health. If the cancer had spread, then they could treat it later with radiation or even chemotherapy. For now, however, they told me that I could go back to a normal life.

At this point Steve Johnson and Steve Kinnard, two dear friends of mine, flew to South Africa from the US to visit and encourage me. I cannot begin to express how much their visit meant to me. Steve Johnson suggested that I should consider getting a second opinion in the States.

I'm sure I looked calm and reasonable on the outside. However, inside I was again very scared. I did not want to reopen this chapter in my life. Steve's advice was excellent though, and as a result, I spent all of January 1996 receiving radiation treatment at Johns Hopkins Hospital in Baltimore, Maryland. Before radiation I had a fifteen percent chance of the cancer recurring. After radiation the experts say I have only a one percent chance of this cancer ever recurring. It would seem that I'm out of the woods. I'm considered cured. Thank God.

What did I learn? Let me start with Mark 2:17:

> *On hearing this, Jesus said to them, "It is not the healthy who need a doctor, but the sick. I have not come to call the righteous, but sinners."*

Obviously, sin is like a deadly disease. It stalks us and seeks to destroy us. It ruins our relationships, steals our joy and robs us of a home in heaven.

The cure for sin is the cross of Jesus Christ. With his death almost 2,000 years ago, he took our sins and our punishment. The penalty that we should have received, he took in our place on that day at Calvary. No one deserves to go to heaven. All of us are guilty of sin, which separates us from God. Indeed, it is we who deserved to hang on that cross. All of us should have died. "For the wages of sin is death..." (Romans 6:23a).

Instead, Jesus paid our penalty.

It's true that Jesus died for all the sins of everyone in the world. But it is also true that everyone on earth is not saved. You must do your part. You must believe in Jesus (John 3:16), repent of your sins (Luke 13:3), become a disciple of Jesus (Matthew 28:18-20) and be baptized for the forgiveness of your sins (Acts 2:38). *You must accept his gospel.*

It's quite simple, really. Sin is the disease. The cross is the cure. Jesus is the doctor. He stands waiting with open arms wanting to help us. He's ready to love us, save us and bless us with abundant life.

One of the biggest problems we face today is that we simply do not want to go to the doctor. We know that Jesus is the answer, but we're in denial. We struggle to see our sins. We struggle to accept our need for God.

I know that some of you who are reading this are thinking about becoming a Christian. You are considering turning your life over to God. You believe in Jesus, but you're saying things like:

"I can't believe I'm lost."

"I have sinned, yes, but I'm no sinner."

"I'm certainly not as bad as so-and-so."

You are in denial, plain and simple. The Bible is telling you, for instance, that it is time to be a disciple or to be baptized, but you are fighting God's Spirit. The Scriptures are showing you that it's time to repent or seek first his kingdom, but you will not accept it. "Certainly I don't need to repent, do I?"

My advice to you here is to stop all the defensiveness and obey the Scriptures. Get honest with yourself and with God.

I understand denial very well. Every cancer patient does. No one wants to accept the fact that he's carrying a tumor which could kill him. In fact, I carried the tumor for over two years, never wanting to believe it could be serious. "Certainly this will heal on its own," I thought. I tried ignoring it. I tried positive thinking. I tried to forget about it. But none of these tactics worked. The tumor was real, and it would not just go away. The truth was that I needed to go to a doctor, but I just did not want to go.

After the first operation I was laying at home recovering. Some friends came by to visit me, and we were talking in the living room when the wife said to me, "You know, my brother had the same kind of cancer as you have."

"Oh really," I replied. "What happened to him?"

"Well," she continued, "He got better for a while. Then the cancer recurred and he died."

"Oh," I mumbled. There was a long silence in the room.

Obviously, this woman is a dear friend of ours, and we laugh about her comment now whenever we all get together. But she stepped over a social boundary line. She crossed some imaginary barrier. Going against what is socially accepted, she prompted me to take down my shields of denial. She reminded me of reality. She reminded me that I am mortal.

When I returned to church in South Africa after my six weeks of treatment in America, a sister came up to me in the fellowship. "Mike," she said. "You're fat now."

In African culture that's a fine comment to make. She meant that I was looking stout and more healthy. Carrying some weight is a sign of prosperity in many African countries.

But just try making that comment at a dinner party in North America. "Hello, Susan. My, my, you've gotten plump lately." It would be totally offensive because, not only are North Americans generally overweight, but we are in denial as well. No one wants to be told the truth. People buy loose-fitting clothes, suck in their guts and go to all lengths to hide it. It is seemingly impossible for some to face the truth.

Denial is a fact of life. And some of us are in spiritual denial. We refuse to accept the reality of our spiritual condition. We try positive thinking. We try to ignore the truth. We try to forget about it. We don't like it when people bring it up. We avoid people who will be blunt with us. We stay away from frank preachers who might prompt us to face the facts. We keep the Bible tightly closed because we know it will call us to change. But listen to how the Bible describes this kind of behavior: "Whoever loves discipline loves knowledge, but he who hates correction is stupid" (Proverbs 12:1).

Let me beg you to stop it. Denial can lead you to hell. Denial can cost you your soul. If you need to repent, then repent. If you need to be baptized, then be baptized. If you need to accept that you are lost, then accept it. What I am saying is that if the Scriptures are telling you something, then do not fight God with your denial. A large part of accepting Jesus is accepting where you really are before God. The Bible is not going to go away. The truth isn't going to disappear simply because you stick your head in the sand. Being honest with yourself is a rare virtue these days. (I'm talking to Christians, as well!)

The apostle Paul warned Timothy about denial. He told him to watch out, because some people will not put up with the truth. They will leave the church and go find some teacher who will make them feel good:

> Preach the Word; be prepared in season and out of season; correct, rebuke and encourage—with great patience and careful instruction. For the time will come when men will not put up with sound doctrine. Instead, to suit their own desires, they will gather around them a great number of teachers to say what their itching ears want to hear. They will turn their ears away from the truth and turn aside to myths. But you, keep your head in all situations, endure hardship, do the work of an evangelist, discharge all the duties of your ministry (2 Timothy 4:2-5).

Denial is deadly. There are lots of people who will tell you "You're okay. Everything's fine. Don't be concerned." But I say that it is good to be concerned. It is good to face the truth about ourselves.

One time in New York a friend of mine was studying the Bible with a young man. He said, "Turn over to Colossians." The young man looked up.

"Colossians?"

"Yes," my friend said. "Let's look at Colossians, chapter two."

The young man began flipping and fanning through the pages trying to find it. He was rather religious and was embarrassed. He did not have the foggiest idea where Colossians was located in the Bible.

Finally he looked up. "Colossians. Hmmm...it must be in my *other* Bible."

We all smile at this today. But it is serious. Rather than just admit that he did not know the Scriptures all that well, he tried to save face.

And here is the crucial point of this chapter: My friend, don't save your face. Save your soul.

Of course, not only those who are thinking of becoming Christians are dealing with denial. Christians can be in spiritual denial, as well. Indeed, denial is one of Satan's favorite tools for extracting you from the body of Christ.

> *The coming of the lawless one will be in accordance with the work of Satan displayed in all kinds of counterfeit miracles, signs and wonders, and in every sort of evil that deceives those who are perishing. They perish because they refuse to love the truth and so be saved (2 Thessalonians 2:9-10).*

Anyone can perish if they refuse to love the truth. Denial can cost you your soul. Listen to Jesus in Matthew 7:21-23:

> *Not everyone who says to me, "Lord, Lord," will enter the kingdom of heaven, but only he who does the will of my Father who is in heaven. Many will say to me on that day, "Lord, Lord, did we not prophesy in your name, and in your name drive out demons and perform many miracles?" Then I will tell them plainly, "I never knew you. Away from me, you evildoers!"*

"Many," it seems, will stand before God thinking that they were great guys. "Many" will think that they had done miracles or prophesied. Jesus, however, will cut through the denial and speak the truth.

"Away from me, you evildoers."

Has your evangelism become lukewarm? Really? Is your marriage a mess? Has it been weeks since you brought a friend to church? Is there immorality in your life? Is it clearly time to repent? Then do not retreat into denial. Rather, get honest with yourself. Open up your heart to God and to the Scriptures, and face the truth.

☩

One morning after my surgeries, I went into the kitchen to fix my breakfast. As I sat down to my bowl of corn flakes, all the emotions of the cancer swept over me. I started to cry. Indeed, I wept. What hit me square in the face was the knowledge that I was going to die. It is something that, four years earlier, I would have agreed with in principle, but not understood emotionally. I love God, and I trust him. But I admit that it was an emotional moment for me when it sank in that my time on this planet is limited.

Cancer has changed me. I know that in the game of life, I am now in the second half. I view my marriage differently. I see my kids differently. I view my chance to tell people about Christ differently. Suddenly, these things have become so much more important to me. But the truth came at a price, and that price was tears. I had to face reality. I had to stop the denial.

And so the truth may be shocking. It may be embarrassing. You may be afraid. There may be false doctors telling you false doctrines about how you are okay and that really nothing is wrong. But if you want to be healed, you must end the denial and face the truth.

Some of you are still acting like the iron man atop Mount Kilimanjaro. You are still acting like there is nothing wrong. But it is time to admit the damage sin has done to your soul. It is time to admit the sin's presence. It is time to admit it to yourself. My victory over cancer came when I decided to go to the doctor. Your victory over sin begins when you get honest with yourself and go to Jesus.

# CHAPTER 4

# Meningitis

*I tell you, now is the time of God's favor,*
*now is the day of salvation.*

2 Corinthians 6:2

# AFRICA

**Accra, GHANA**

**O**yinda had everything an African woman could wish for. Although born in Nigeria, she was raised and educated in England. She had a degree in accounting, a fine job in London and was enjoying life as a disciple in the church in London.

In 1989 that church sent a small group of Christians to Nigeria to begin a congregation in Lagos. Oyinda was an obvious choice to be invited as a team member. She was a strong Christian woman known for her character and devotion to God. While millions of Africans from Cape Town to Dakar are plotting and scheming to find passage to the West, here was a woman who was wanting to go against the crowd. She was ready to brave the heat, crime, corruption and illness of Africa in order to help bring light to our continent. Although the daughter of a prominent family, there was no trace of snobbery in her. Oyinda had a way of making everyone feel comfortable and at ease.

She immediately stood out in the Lagos church. Without an ounce of materialism, she flourished in an environment where others would have fallen apart. She married Dolapo Ogundipe in 1992, and in 1994 they moved to Ghana to direct the church in the capital city of Accra. When the Accra Christian Church quickly became one of the fastest growing churches in our movement, it was no surprise to anyone, except perhaps for Oyinda. Her humility accepted both success and defeat with a faithful calm which endeared her to all who knew her. She was at once a tough and a gentle lady.

Dolapo and Oyinda had a three-bedroom cottage in Accra which became a "Grand Central Station" for the church. People came and went constantly. Amazingly, the church actually *quadrupled* in size within twenty months. Such was the powerful leadership of Dolapo and Oyinda through the power of God's Spirit. Their son Ope was born in 1994.

Life was so different in Accra from the one Oyinda had left behind in London. There are no movie theaters and only a few hygienically sound restaurants. There are no Western-style shopping malls. The electricity works well, and the roads are passable, but crime is bad. The equatorial heat is stifling. And when it rains, the rains come so forcefully that you would almost expect Noah's ark to float by.

However, never once did I hear Oyinda or Dolapo lament their decision to embrace the challenges of life in Africa. They were so devoted to their vision of a Ghana won for Christ, I doubt they spent any time at all complaining.

Those of us who have worked in Africa all have our stories to tell. We have all gotten sick here. I had cancer. My wife almost died giving birth to Nathan in Abidjan (she lost half her blood.) Our church leaders have had typhoid, malaria, dysentery, food poisoning and hepatitis.

Four countries where we have churches are currently embroiled in civil war. All of us have seen rioting. Serena Dieng caught the last plane out of Liberia before the rebels stormed the airport. I have been tear gassed twice and the Fleurants, who work in Ivory Coast, and Oguaghas, who work in Nigeria, were on a plane that almost crashed in the jungles of Cameroon.

When we do all get together, we inevitably stay up late trading stories about our different experiences on the continent. The stories seem to get bigger and bigger as the years go by.

We all knew when we came to Africa in 1989 that anything could happen. Africa is not only poor, but it is dangerous. Yet it still came as a shock when our dear sister Oyinda came down with meningitis.

Surrounding the brain and spinal cord is a layer of tissue and fluids called the "meninges." This tissue serves to both nourish and protect the brain. Meningitis occurs when the fluids become infected with either a virus or bacteria. Soon the meninges themselves become red and swollen. The fluid, which is normally crystal clear, becomes cloudy. The infection then moves rapidly into the brain.

Meningitis has become rare in Europe and America. Outbreaks are usually contained quickly by health care professionals. The viral form is serious but usually not fatal. Often the patient can recover fully in a few weeks. It is a bacterial form of meningitis, however, which is most dangerous. Called "meningococcal meningitis," it is a serious and life-threatening disease. In Africa, where oftentimes a person's resistance to disease is lower because of the poor nutrition, meningitis kills thousands of people every year. As I write these words, there is an epidemic raging through West Africa.

The first symptom of meningitis is a severe headache often accompanied by vomiting. As the meninges become more irritated, a stiff neck develops. Often the patient will avoid any bright light as the bacteria attacks the nerves in the eyes. Convulsions may follow; then a coma.

The great danger of meningitis is the speed at which it works. People can die in as little as twelve hours, even with the best of medical care. The most accurate diagnosis is made as the result of the lumbar puncture. The doctor actually draws fluid straight from the meninges. If it is cloudy, he will immediately prescribe massive doses of antibiotics. If the disease is caught quickly enough, the patient has a fighting chance. Survival rates in Africa are about fifty percent. Delay means that the disease will quickly take your life. Immediate action is mandatory. Dealing with meningitis is all about urgency.

On a Monday in August 1996, Oyinda came down with flu-like symptoms which she thought was malaria. She was feverish and had a severe headache. She took some anti-malarial medicine and rested at home. Tuesday came and she felt no better; in fact, she felt worse. Dolapo took her to a nearby hospital and checked her in. The doctors gave her a blood test for typhoid fever which came back positive. Immediately they began giving her antibiotics to cure the illness. Ironically, she probably did have typhoid, but the symptoms were masking the deeper problem of meningitis.

By Wednesday Dolapo was complaining to the doctor about how Oyinda was not improving. The doctor re-examined her and found Oyinda to be suffering from a stiff neck and over-sensitivity to light—the classic signs of meningitis. Since she was already on antibiotics, he simply noted his findings and did not change the treatment.

Thursday found Oyinda somewhat better. She sat up in bed with some help and was joking and talking with some Christians who came to visit her. She ate and poked fun at her friends. She seemed to be turning the corner. By Saturday, however, she was much worse. Oyinda was concerned and asked Dolapo to move her to another Accra hospital where a specialist would begin to treat her.

On Saturday evening the doctor finally released her so that she could be transferred to the other hospital. In the taxi (no ambulances were available), Dolapo told her to rest as they drove through the city. She was afraid to sleep. She said, "I'm afraid I will never wake up."

The specialist saw her at 10:00 p.m. She obviously had meningitis, and she urgently needed massive dosages of antibiotics. The doctor must have known that she was near death. He finished quickly and went down the hall to get some medicine. After he left Dolapo stayed with Oyinda in her room. He talked to her for a while, holding her hand. He told her that he loved her as he searched for encouraging words. A vague fear was welling up inside of him. She was not able to say much. At one point he was in mid-sentence when he turned toward her. He noticed with alarm that her pupils had dilated. She had slipped into a coma. He called for the nurses who came rushing in. As he watched his wife laying on the bed, he suddenly realized that she was no longer breathing.

It was all over. She was gone.

Dolapo went out into the darkened hallway. Standing there all alone, he put his hands to his face and turned toward the wall. He thought about his two-year-old son whose memories of his mother would soon begin to fade. He thought about family members who must be notified. He felt the deep anguish at the loss of his beloved friend and companion. As the huge lump in his chest rose up into his throat, he began to pray. "God you are awesome," he said. "If I can accept the good, then I can accept the bad. God you are awesome." Then he broke down and wept.

In some ways, the pain and sadness of losing Oyinda cannot be cured. Time is helpful, of course. We learn how to manage our grief. The pain seems to lessen. And yet there will always be a hole in our hearts left behind by Oyinda.

However, the certainty of the resurrection is powerful. At her funeral in Ghana, Steve Johnson remarked: "As terrible a loss as this may be, remember that Oyinda would not trade places with any of us."

She had gone home to be with God. Although in our human eyes she left us early, the goal of every man and woman should be to follow in her footsteps. Oyinda fought the good fight. She wears the crown of glory.

✠

But what lesson do we need to learn from the meningitis that took her life? I would suggest that we need to learn the lesson of urgency and apply it to our spiritual lives.

We often live in a fog. Materialism and sin infect our brains. We see things like our jobs, our houses or the size of our car as vitally important. We fail to recognize the reality of spiritual matters. We fail to grasp the fact that there is a heaven, a hell and a judgment day swiftly approaching. When you stand before God to be judged, it will not matter whether you drove a

Porsche or took the bus. It will not matter whether you were a company president or a street sweeper. The only thing that will matter at that moment is whether you have been saved from sin by the blood of Jesus Christ.

We must therefore be urgent about our salvation. We must be urgent about the sin which can destroy us. We must act quickly to repent of the evil which can take us out of the race, steal our crown and rob us of glory. We never know when a fast-moving illness or a car accident or some other unexpected event may end our lives on earth and usher us into eternity.

If you have been a Christian for some time, or if you are only considering becoming one, my plea is to be urgent about the sin which stalks you. Sin is a killer which is working hard to infect and destroy you. And sin will work more quickly than you suspect to harden your heart, turn your head and lead you down the broad road to destruction.

My belief is that Oyinda would certainly beg you to be urgent. This was her message when she was with us. It would be even more her message now. The clock is ticking. Now is your chance to be open about sin, repent of it, and go on to glory. Now is not the time to dilly-dally around.

First of all, urgency demands we call sin by its real name and stop using cute little euphemisms. For example Galatians 5:19 reads:

*The acts of the sinful nature are obvious: sexual immorality, impurity, and debauchery.*

Notice how sexual immorality ("fornication" is the word used by the older versions) is a sin. How men and women cringe at the words "adultery" and "immorality"! Instead, people "have a fling," "fool around," "have an affair," "sleep together," "mess around," "make love," or describe sin in other ways that do not sound that bad. "Fornication," "adultery" and "immorality" don't seem to apply anymore.

However, just because you put an innocuous sugar-coated name on your sin does not mean that God will turn a blind eye. Just the opposite. God describes sexual immorality as a horrible act in the Scriptures. We must avoid it (Acts 15:29), put it to death (Colossians 3:5), flee from it (1 Corinthians 6:18), and not even have a hint of it (Ephesians 5:3). The immoral gain only God's wrath (Colossians 3:6), and they lose their places in heaven (Ephesians 5:5; Galatians 5:21). Proverbs 5 connects immorality to all of the following words: "bitter," "death," "the grave," "folly" and "utter ruin." Proverbs 6 speaks with similar clarity:

> Can a man scoop fire into his lap
>     without his clothes being burned?
> Can a man walk on hot coals
>     without his feet being scorched?
> So is he who sleeps with another man's wife;
>     no one who touches her will go unpunished
>     (Proverbs 6: 27-29).

> But a man who commits adultery lacks judgment;
>     whoever does so destroys himself.

*Blows and disgrace are his lot,*
    *and his shame will never be wiped away.*
    *(Proverbs 6:32-33).*

It is obvious that our cute little syrupy names cannot cover up the horrible sin of adultery and fornication. Just as it is foolishness to call meningitis the flu, it is equally foolish to call fornication a fling.

I remember as a child being given a medicine I had to swallow. I took a glass of water and tried to gulp it down. The pill, however, was too big, and I kept gagging on it. Finally, I decided that it could not taste as bad as all that. I put the pill between my teeth and bit down hard, chewing it in my mouth. Immediately my tongue informed my brain of the disgusting taste exploding behind my lips. Making a face, I stuck out my tongue and quickly rinsed my mouth. I did not appreciate raw medicine without the sugar coating. I simply could not handle the straight stuff.

Some of us are still acting like children when it comes to spiritual matters. We are still babies. We cannot handle straight talk about sin. We still shy away from honestly calling the sin by its real, biblical name. We love our sugar coatings. We hate to say we lied. Instead we say we "weren't totally honest." We did not steal something, but just "borrowed it." We did not gossip; we just confided. We did not lust; we just gave her the "once over." We were never racists. We just do not believe that "those people" are as good as we are.

The list is as endless as the point is obvious. Sin needs to be dealt with quickly and decisively. Don't waste precious time trying to fool yourself and others with all the fancy sugar-coated euphemisms. Urgency demands honesty.

Second, urgency demands that we take action to repent, and not just feel something. In 2 Corinthians 7, Paul talks to the Corinthian church about true repentance. He compares godly sorrow with worldly sorrow. Godly sorrow is an eager, earnest change of behavior. It is not complicated. You simply repent with all your heart. Worldly sorrow is a long-faced sadness without the victory of repentance. Let's walk through the passage.

> *Even if I caused you sorrow by my letter, I do not regret it. Though I did regret it—I see that my letter hurt you, but only for a little while (2 Corinthians 7:8).*

Paul notes, in reference to his first letter to the Corinthian church, that his letter stung the church emotionally. Indeed, we know that the truth hurts. 2 Corinthians 7:9 reads:

> *...yet now I am happy, not because you were made sorry, but because your sorrow led you to repentance. For you became sorrowful as God intended and so were not harmed in any way by us.*

Paul says that he is happy that he spoke strong, uncompromising and convicting words to them because in the end they repented.

*Godly sorrow brings repentance that leads to salvation and leaves no regret, but worldly sorrow brings death (2 Corinthians 7 :10).*

Worldly sorrow brings death. Crying, feeling guilty, or having a long face makes no difference. The goal is repentance.

*See what this godly sorrow has produced in you: what earnestness, what eagerness to clear yourselves, what indignation, what alarm, what longing, what concern, what readiness to see justice done. At every point you have proved yourselves to be innocent in this matter (2 Corinthians 7:11).*

So, what is repentance? Paul spells it out for us. Allow me to include some dictionary definitions.

*Earnestness:* "Seriousness in mind and sincerity of intention." This person has every intention of changing. His mind is focused on repentance.

*Eagerness:* "Impatiently desirous of, anxious or avid." This person's intentions are clear and strong. With all his heart he wants to change.

*Indignation:* "Anger aroused by something felt to be...wrong." Indignation is a righteous anger. He does not wring his hands and limply say that he hopes he someday changes. Indignation stands up, clenches his teeth, makes a fist and cries out, "Never again!"

*Alarm:* "Fear or terror aroused by awareness of danger." True repentance sees and feels the danger of sin. It is never complacent like Felix (Acts 24:25) or simply remorseful like Judas (Matthew 27:3). Repentance must act, and act quickly, to make it right.

Too many people today substitute good intentions or guilty feelings in the place of repentance. Others substitute tears, regret or sadness. We must, however, face the facts. A long face, sorrowful feelings and empty promises are no substitute for repentance.

Sometimes I speak with leaders who need to hear this point. Asked why their ministries are not growing, some respond with "woe is me" hand wringing, a long face and vague excuses about "my situation." I also speak to disciples from time to time who neglect the basics of the faith. Their evangelism has drifted through mediocrity and into oblivion. They do little or nothing for the poor. Their marriages are weak. Usually when we are in this situation, we know we need to change. We have heard sermons about it. We have read the Scriptures. But instead of truly repenting, we stop short. We cheat ourselves out of the joy of true Christianity, substituting a Judas-like remorse in the place of true repentance. Instead of indignation and alarm, we find a vague guilt and a long face. Instead of earnestness and eagerness, our friends see crocodile tears and good intentions. This is no formula for joy.

Acts 3:19 tells us that repentance brings us times of refreshing! If you are not refreshed, ask yourself if you have truly repented. If you do not enjoy living the Christian life anymore, maybe it is because you are not living the *Christian* life anymore. The Bible, however, cuts through all of our weaving and dodging and commands us to repent of our sins immediately and with indignation.

Once at a friend's house we were enjoying a cookout. As the children swam in the pool at the far end of the yard, I noticed something strange about my youngest son, Joshua. Indeed, I could not see him. I could only make out a dark shape in the deeper water. His head was not coming up. Immediately, my earnestness became eagerness which grew instantly into alarm. As I sprinted across the grass, I realized that Joshua was drowning. Although I reached him easily and pulled him out, I quickly felt a deep indignation about what I had done. Never again would I allow another close call. This would never happen again! That is repentance. Not some spineless intention, but a strong decision.

Are you ready to repent of your sins? Are you eager and indignant? Do you feel the terror of godly alarm? Can you hear the voice of urgency? Or rather, have you allowed the spiritual meningitis the time it needs to multiply in your system? Have you given the bacteria the room to operate, treating the deadly disease as if it would simply go away tomorrow?

Urgency calls you to strip off the nice names and syrupy labels which we give to sin. It begs us to call the sin by its proper name. It calls us to listen carefully to our brothers and sisters who are helping us to see it. Urgency also calls us to have godly sorrow about our sin. Remorse, guilt or good intentions simply do not suffice. Urgency pleads for true repentance...an eagerness, indignation and alarm about the sin in our lives.

Some of us in Africa have learned from a painful personal experience that meningitis cuts you down quickly. It is not a head cold, the flu or some little bug. It moves to destroy you. Meningitis can kill you within twelve hours, even if you are lying in a first-world hospital which quickly identifies the disease.

Meningitis is an urgent, unflinching and indiscriminate killer. Sin is equally dangerous. We dare not take it lightly. Too often have I seen Christians slip into spiritual comas because of the sin they refused to take seriously. Too often have I spoken to people who had regrets, but no repentance.

Let us, therefore, become urgent about sin. Let us diagnose it accurately, and then let us take strong steps to eradicate it.

Can you hear the voice of Urgency?

Can you hear the voice of Oyinda?

# CHAPTER 5

# Tetanus

*When I kept silent,*
*my bones wasted away.*

Psalm 32:3

# AFRICA

● Duékoue, GABON

"Clostridium tetani" is virtually everywhere. Found in the dirt and dust, it is on thorns and rusty nails, as well. It sits there in our environment as harmless as a kitten. You cannot see or smell it. You would never even think twice about it.

It is altogether another story when the bacteria enters your body. Unable to multiply where there is a constant flow of blood, it usually is not a threat to your health. But in the case of a deep puncture wound where damaged flesh loses its steady blood supply, the bacteria begins to multiply quickly. As it grows, this bacteria produces a toxin quite lethal to humans, which soon brings on the disease called "tetanus" (sometimes called "lockjaw").

Tetanus is rare in North America. With most people effectively immunized, the bulk of the population is protected. Africa, however, is a different story. Millions are vulnerable to the disease and thousands die from it each year.

The disease attacks the nervous system. A common first sign is muscular stiffness in the jaw, followed by stiffness in the neck, difficulty in swallowing, spasms, sweating and fever. Once infected, you may wait anywhere from three days to one month for the first symptoms to occur. Generally, the shorter incubation periods are associated with the more heavily contaminated wounds. Once the symptoms have begun, your chances of survival are fifty-fifty. Treatment includes antitoxins and antibiotics. In many African countries, however, because precious time is often lost in going to the witch doctor, survival rates are far lower. The horror of tetanus, though long forgotten in the West, hangs over Africa like a treacherous storm cloud.

Marcelle Deh grew up in the small town of Duékoue in western Ivory Coast. In the 1970s, Duékoue was still very remote and lacking a sophisticated infrastructure. There were no paved roads or traffic lights. Many lit their homes with oil lanterns, and few had phones or piped water. It is a beautiful area, with lush forests covering the rolling mountains all the way to the Liberian border. Days are hot. Nights are cool. What the people lacked in economic success, they more than made up for in warmth and hospitality.

One afternoon in 1974, Marcelle's mother asked her to run to the shop down the street from her home in the center of town. Barefoot, she stepped onto the dirt road in front of her house. Like most eight-year-olds, she walked and skipped down the street without a care in the world. She soon turned a corner and passed the town clinic.

It was dry season at the time. The red dirt was crusty and cracked. Suddenly a sharp pain in her foot made her cry out. Looking down she saw what seemed to be a fish bone sticking solidly into her foot. In stepping on it she had jammed the bone deep into her flesh. Although standing literally in front of the town clinic, like any eight-year-old, she limped home crying to mama, without even stopping to pull out the bone.

Her mother could hear Marcelle coming and met her at the door. Laying her on the old sofa, she examined her foot. Then she yanked out the fish bone and discovered that it was not a fish bone at all. Rather, she was shocked to see that her daughter had stepped on a rusty syringe. Frightened, Mama picked up her daughter and marched straight back to the clinic.

Since it was Sunday, there was no doctor present in the emergency area. Only a few nurses were on duty, and they were all fairly busy. After a long wait, Marcelle finally received attention. Although her mother explained about the rusty syringe, the nurse only managed to clean the wound and bandage the little girl before being called to the next patient. Marcelle received no tetanus shot and no warning. Obviously, she had no idea of the danger she faced. She walked home that day feeling that her ordeal was over. Little did she know that the bacteria was already beginning to multiply at a deadly pace.

Several days later, Marcelle developed what she thought was a sore throat. Strangely enough, she not only had difficulty swallowing, but she was having difficulty moving her jaw at all. Her throat felt heavy and thick. Everyone assumed it would all clear up. But her condition worsened.

One night when her father came home from work, she tried to get up to greet him. Instead, she found that she could not stand. She could only crawl toward the door in order to give him a hug and a kiss. Her back and facial muscles were beginning to spasm, and movement was becoming awkward.

The sight of his daughter in this condition startled the father. That night he brought over the witch doctor to see about fixing her illness. Later he arrived in full regalia: beads, skins and headdress. The witch doctor sat on the floor and tossed down some bones. He stared at them for a long time before speaking. The bones told him that someone had cast a spell on the daughter and that she needed both protection and healing. He gave her a fetish for protection and some herbs to use in healing. For this "service" he charged one week's salary and a chicken, which he promised to sacrifice later to appease the spirits. He took the money and then ate the chicken. Marcelle's condition promptly deteriorated. Her mother had seen enough. Two days later she checked her into the clinic.

The examining doctor quickly diagnosed her illness and began to treat it properly. By this time, however, the spasms were turning into full-blown tetanus. Her jaw would lock shut. Her facial muscles would freeze into an eerie smile, and she looked much like the joker in the Batman movie. Doctors call this the "ris sardonicus," or "sardonic smile." Her spine would arch and her arms would lock. At one point three adults tried to straighten her arms but could not. Some victims actually suffer a fracture of the spine and broken long bones. Such is the power of the spasms. Breathing becomes difficult. Eating is impossible. Although the little girl was fully conscious, she could not speak during the spasms. The spasms would come and go in waves, leaving her exhausted and terrified. She was in danger of slipping into a coma and dying. Sadly, the hospital put her in a room with a view of the city morgue. All day long she watched the workers unload stiff corpses coming in from the villages near by. The irony did not escape her. She despaired of life. Her mother simply sat by the bed and fell apart emotionally.

Throughout Africa the problem of how to feed a tetanus patient is solved in a variety of ways. Some Kenyan tribes break off the front teeth of all their children. With the large gap in the teeth they are able to insert a straw to feed them should they contract the disease. Marcelle had the more advanced IV drip. This was the best solution, but she still lost a great deal of weight.

Oddly enough, when her muscles froze during the spasms, Marcelle felt no pain. Locked into the strange position, she felt only panic as the spasms gripped her entire body. She would try to speak and call out, but the most she could manage was to make a slight noise. The powerful spasms continued for two or three weeks. Several times it seemed that death was near. Her parents had resigned themselves to the fact that the little girl would die any day. But somehow the eight-year-old hung on to life. Staring out the window at the morgue below, with sweat pouring down her face, she stubbornly refused to give up the fight. Gasping for breath during the waves of paralysis, she bravely clung to consciousness. In the stifling heat and one-hundred percent humidity of West Africa, she somehow summoned the strength to survive.

One day she realized that the spasms were becoming less frequent. Her body was actually beginning to win its war against the tetanus bacteria. Each passing day brought less and less of the horror of the disease. Within two months she was actually on her feet and fully recovered. The little girl was certainly a fighter. Starting with a big grin on her face, she eventually cried as she walked out of the hospital. Then instead of turning left toward the morgue, she turned right and headed down the dusty street toward home. This time she was sure to wear her shoes.

Today Marcelle is strong and healthy, a Bible discussion leader in the Abidjan church. Although she escaped with her life, she still remembers the terror of lockjaw. She'll never forget wanting so badly to speak and move, but not being able to do so. And her mother will never forget that eerie smile. It was the "sardonic smile" that scared her nearly to death.

✝

I firmly believe that tetanus illustrates all too well one of our greatest dangers as Christians. If Satan can simply get us to shut our mouths and close up our hearts, he knows that we will fall soon enough. Honest conversation with other Christians is as vital to our spiritual health as breathing is to our bodies. If Satan can stop us from being open, confessing our sin and sharing our problems with others, then he has mortally wounded us. Christianity was never meant to be lived alone. It was always God's plan for the church to be a group of people who helped one another. Spiritual lockjaw is a threat to our survival as disciples. We must open our mouths and be honest with one another in order to grow up quickly in Jesus.

Spiritual tetanus begins with a wound. Many times I have seen Christians who were wronged inadvertently by a brother or sister who perhaps said something offensive, gave some bad advice or was not friendly in some situation. The Christian feels wounded. He believes he was slighted. She begins to harbor a grudge or a bad attitude. He might even become disillusioned with the church itself. "How can this be the movement of God when no one called me when I was sick?" she grumbles. The more he thinks about it, the more angry he becomes.

Sure, he is throwing an immature pity party, but it happens to many of us. "Why didn't he notice me?" "Why didn't she greet me?" "I wasn't invited!" All these comments signify that we have been wounded. Our feelings have gotten hurt. We are a little emotional about it. It is a spiritual test that confronts every Christian: Can you be wronged and still act like Jesus? In this situation, the Bible outlines what we must do. If you wrong me in some way, then I must go immediately to you and sort it out. Matthew states it clearly:

> *"If your brother sins against you, go and show him his fault, just between the two of you. If he listens to you, you have won your brother over" (Matthew 18:15).*

If I have been wronged, then I need to quickly speak to the one who offended me in order to resolve it.

Of course, the reverse is true as well. If I know that I have offended *you*, then Jesus commands me to quickly go and re-solve our differences. Matthew 5:23-24 reads:

> *"Therefore, if you are offering your gift at the altar and there remember that your brother has something against you, leave your gift there in front of the altar. First go and be reconciled to your brother; then come and offer your gift."*

So whether I offended you or was offended by you, I have the obligation to sort out our differences immediately, and so do you. Indeed, Ephesians 4:26 says we should do this before the sun goes down: "Do not let the sun go down while you are still angry."

Whenever conflict arises between two Christians, they should literally bump into one another in the fellowship as they rush to settle their differences. Do not be naive. Conflict will arise. Indeed, the only churches that have no conflict are churches with a membership of one. If you are attending a congregation with two or more members, eventually there will be a conflict in a relationship with another Christian. So the point here is not *if* conflict will occur in your Christian life, but rather, *how* you will deal with it when it does arrive. Rest assured, conflict is a fact of life.

Several years ago I was visiting a US church and sleeping at night in the lead evangelist's study. I happened to be visiting during a staff meeting. My things were stashed in the study while we all met in his living room. During the meeting a brother brought up how another leader would soon be visiting their congregation. "Did we want to have him sleep in the study as well?"

"Oh, no," my friend responded. "I'd never put him in my study. Let's get him a nice hotel room."

No one else noticed, but for some reason I allowed that comment to sting a little. Like a pinprick, my feelings were hurt a tiny bit. *I could sleep in the study,* I thought, *but this other brother gets a nice hotel. Hmmm.* Before me lay two choices. I could allow the tetanus to creep into my veins, or I could resolve this quickly like Jesus would. I decided that moment that it was obviously a sign of our friendship that he let me into his home in the first place and that I was being oversensitive. I did, however, share my feelings with my friend, and he quickly apologized. The matter was forgotten. Today we laugh about it.

Spiritual tetanus, however, is no laughing matter. Many of us have it running through our veins. Our jaws are locked; we will not be open, and the "ris sardonicus" is rigidly in place. Our phony smile says that everything is okay. Meanwhile, toxic attitudes are destroying us within. As bitterness grows, our relationship with God dissolves. It does not really make sense, yet I see it all the time. People leave God because someone offended them in some way. They wear their fake smiles all the way to their spiritual graves, instead of working it out as the Bible commands.

Many times I have seen someone suffer through food poisoning. It is awful. It is a wretched twelve hours before the person starts to feel better. But never have I seen someone giving up eating because of it! Obviously it is ridiculous to give up eating because of one bad dish. In the same way, it is silly to give up God and his people because of one bad experience. Yet, people do it all the time.

A relative of mine was leaving her church when the minister made some crass and inappropriate remark. It offended my relative and caused her to stop going to church at all. She would bring it up from time to time in conversation. Reliving the moment, she would stoke the fires of her bitterness and anger.

Tetanus seized her like a vice grip. She wouldn't dream of going back to the minister and asking for an apology. She refused to hear any talk of forgiveness. Indeed, this event happened in the 1940s! Yet for five decades she held on to her grudge with tight fists and white knuckles. I do not doubt that the minister's comment was inappropriate. But being emotional and stubborn about it is just as inappropriate.

And so I say that spiritual tetanus is deadly. If you refuse to open your mouth and resolve your conflicts, you simply will not survive. Young or old as a disciple, if you shut your mouth and plaster a fake smile onto your face, your days in the kingdom are numbered.

What can you do to avoid spiritual tetanus? First of all, stop taking everything so personally. I feel sorry for the Christian who is put under the microscope by his brother or sister in the Lord. Some become hypersensitive and totally self-focused. "You didn't greet me. You didn't invite me. You like them more than me." This immature pity party soon leads to dislike and anger. Hebrews 12 warns us clearly about these bitter roots in our lives:

> *See to it that no one misses the grace of God and that no bitter root grows up to cause trouble and defile many (Hebrews 12:15).*

We must dig up these bitter roots and destroy them, or else they will destroy us.

Second, admit it when someone hurts your feelings, and go resolve it. Pry open your locked jaw, and confront the one who offended you. Otherwise, it will poison your friendship. If he is wrong, the conversation will help him in the future to be more Christlike. If you are wrong, then you can apologize and be done with the matter. Sometimes I start a conversation by saying, "I might be a little sensitive here, but something you said hurt my feelings." Of course, sometimes I am clearly being wronged and sinned against. Here I state my feelings directly, yet always with an eye toward resolving the conflict and not just winning a battle.

Third, watch out for those long conversations alone with yourself when you are venting your anger and "winning" some argument with another Christian. Remember that you always sound convincing to yourself when you are rehearsing a disagreement. Rather, be sure to give the other person the chance to apologize and to repent. Do not just talk to yourself. Talk to him. And remember that once he has had a chance to explain his side, he may make complete sense.

In any case, guard yourself against spiritual tetanus. It seeks to shut your mouth and multiply the toxins of bitterness within you. Poor little Marcelle was unable to move or open her mouth during her spasms. The disease gripped her like an anaconda. You, however, have an advantage. You can open your mouth. You can speak. With the help of God's Spirit, you can open up and destroy the killer within.

✠

Sometimes we suffer from a different form of spiritual tetanus. Our mouth is locked shut, our heart is sealed tight and we refuse to discuss the problem. Yet, the problem is not with another Christian. Sometimes it is a sin which has wounded us spiritually. After we have committed a sin, at times we simply do not want to repent of it. Instead, we give in to the temptation of hiding the sin and acting like everything is okay. We continue to come to church and smile as always, yet deep down inside the sin is destroying us.

Of course, it would be so easy to sit down with a close friend and confess the sin plaguing us. God's plan is that we help one another to overcome our obstacles. But the shame of our sin and our proud concern for how we look sometimes pushes us to do things that are stupid. We shut our mouths, allowing the toxins of bitterness, guilt and shame to multiply. Some plaster a fake smile on their faces and avoid honest conversation. Others look glum and start missing church services. Spiritual tetanus is deadly, and I have seen some Christians leave God altogether at this point. They simply feel guilty about the hypocritical double life they have been living. Spiritual tetanus has locked their mouths shut, and they refuse to open them. James 5:16 is a great passage on this topic:

*Therefore confess your sins to each other and pray for each other so that you may be healed. The prayer of a righteous man is powerful and effective.*

In Christ we have the beautiful opportunity of sitting down with a brother or sister and being open about our mistakes. First, we receive the benefits of the prayers of a close friend. Second, we hear some good advice about how we can avoid the sin in the future. Third, we receive some encouragement that we can change, that we can win the victory and that we can put the matter behind us. Obviously, the blessings of confession are enormous. The deadly lockjaw is so easy to defeat. All we have to do is open our mouths and be honest. And then Satan scampers away, defeated again in his attempt to destroy us.

> *Submit yourselves, then, to God. Resist the devil, and he will flee from you (James 4:7).*

This beautiful and simple plan of God, however, is often foiled by our pride. Rather than repenting and moving on, we hide the sin and act like nothing is wrong. So it is *we* who are defeated!

While my wife and I were living in Kenya, "Andrew" (not his real name) was baptized into Christ. He was a pastor from Tanzania who had a few churches under his charge. He seemed zealous for God and quickly helped a few people to become biblical disciples. I was happy to see his growth, and within a few months I asked him to join our full-time ministry staff as an intern-trainee. He accepted immediately.

My wife was the first one to sense that something was wrong. I don't know exactly what tipped her off, but she began to feel uncomfortable about him. He was a little "unreal," a little too spiritual. There was something phony about his demeanor. I started praying that God would work in this situation.

Well, God worked.

Later on, some Christians living near Andrew saw him out walking one night. As they approached him to say hello, he actually turned and entered the house of a prostitute. (Obviously, he had not seen the disciples.) They were shocked that he had gone into the well-known brothel. The next day they confronted him. Andrew at first got angry and denied everything. But as they talked on, he finally admitted it all. He had been going to prostitutes for months. His shame had kept him from confessing it and repenting.

As it turned out, he was not so much sorry for his sins as he was sorry that he had gotten caught. He never came to church again. Sadly, the tetanus had cut him down.

I was, to say the least, quite stung by it all. We had prayed together, shared our faith together and had even traveled together out to some remote villages to preach to some of his satellite congregations. All the while he was living a lie. Many times I wondered if I was to blame in some way. In the end, however, I learned a great lesson: Some are addicted to looking good. They would rather leave Jesus than confess their sin and repent.

How about you? Are there sins that you have hidden over which you cannot seem to win the victory? Do you slap on the fake smile every time you go to church? Are your shame and pride keeping you from getting the help you need? Is your fear of confession killing you spiritually? I am not talking just to young Christians here, either. I have seen church leaders fall flat on their faces because they refused to open their mouths and get help. Young and old alike are susceptible to the lockjaw bacteria. I beg you—get help before it is too late!

Someone might ask, "Do I have to confess *every* sin?"

Of course not. You cannot even remember every sin. And who would want to sit there for hours to listen to your long confession! Confession is a valuable help in situations where we are not winning the victory. It helps us to have the prayers and counsel of a friend in those situations where we're not overcoming.

When someone asks, "Do I have to confess?" I say that that's a dumb question. Confession is not something you *have* to do. It is something you *get* to do. It is a privilege that we have in Christ.

People display their immaturity when they ask if they have to confess. That is like asking, "Do I have to bathe regularly?" or "Do I have to brush my teeth?" Obviously, the answer is no. But you have to wonder about the guy who asked the question. My five-year-old son hates to bathe and brush his teeth. As we mature, we realize what a privilege it is to have that opportunity. It is the same with confession. Spiritual babies are the ones who ask if they "have" to confess. Older Christians realize (or should by now) what a joy it is to sit down and have an honest conversation with a sibling in Christ.

Simply put, confession is a great weapon in your struggle against sin. Satan, however, desperately wants you to face this struggle unarmed. He wants you to stand before him without any help, encouragement or advice. He rejoices when you cover up your sin or nurse a long-standing grudge. He hates the thought of you exchanging encouragement and hearing wise counsel from those who have been in the battle for several years. He wants you all alone, discouraged, dismayed and trembling. Satan's plan is to infect your body with pride and lock your mouth so tightly that you will not cry out for help. He longs to see the seizures of guilt and bitterness. He loves the sardonic smile. He knows that you cannot survive very long. Indeed, if spiritual lockjaw has set in, the vultures are probably circling overhead already.

My plea is that you will open your mouth and speak honestly to a brother or sister who can help you. If you would only pull someone aside and be open about your life, then you would experience the encouragement, the help and the clear thinking that open conversations bring. Then a true and heartfelt smile will return to your lips as you once again face the joys and challenges of the Christian life with a clear conscience. Your enemy will slither out the back door, defeated once again.

# CHAPTER 6

# Guinea Worm

*Immediately, because Herod
did not give praise to God, an angel of the Lord
struck him down, and he was eaten
by worms and died.*

Acts 12:23

# AFRICA

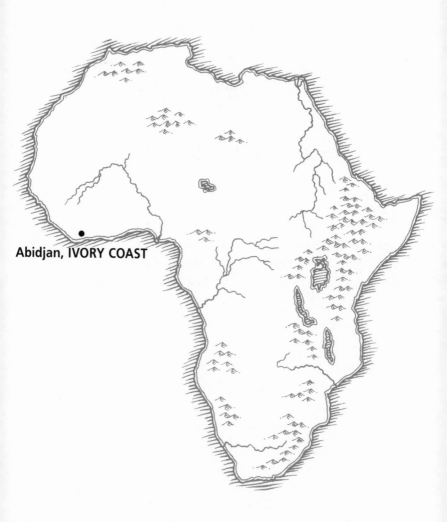

Abidjan, IVORY COAST

Francois Kra grew up in the lush eastern region of the Ivory Coast in West Africa. As a small boy in the 1960s, Francois lived in a village close to the Ghanaian border. Life was fairly simple for the energetic little ten-year-old. His days were filled with school, friends and adventure in the thick forests near his home.

During a school break in 1963 one of Francois' friends asked him if he would be interested in a small job on a nearby cocoa plantation. It all seemed so easy and harmless. The farmer was hiring young village boys to guard his cocoa trees from the hungry squirrels which raided his groves each day. All that the boys had to do was simply walk through the plantation, and scare away the squirrels with stones and shouts. He accepted the job immediately, of course. Rural Africa was quite poor in the 1960s. Electricity and running water were only then becoming available to a small number of villages. Francois was happy for any extra income he could generate for his family.

The plantation was like the Garden of Eden. There were rows and rows of cocoa trees to patrol, and it was fun throwing stones at the squirrels. It almost seemed like he was being paid to play.

Around the edge of the plantation, grew all kinds of other fruit trees. There were coconuts, mangoes and bananas. Cola trees grew there also. He could grab a cola nut almost at will, if he so desired. The mildly addictive nuts are sold all over Equatorial Africa. The effect when sucked on is similar to that from a strong cup of espresso.

As the sun climbed higher in the African sky each day, the temperature would easily reach into the 90s (F), with one-hundred percent humidity. Inevitably Francois would get hot and tired. If he wanted water, he was told to make the long walk back to the well to draw some water. On the far side of the plantation, however, was an outcropping of rocks. There in the shade, rainwater would catch in the rocks in small pools about the size of a shoe box. It was this stagnant water that some of the boys began drinking. At first Francois did not want to taste it. He watched in fear as the other boys went ahead. He himself kept trekking across the plantation to draw from the well. Eventually, he began to rationalize, however, that everyone was drinking it, and surely it couldn't be all that bad. One hot afternoon after first lowering his defenses, he then lowered his face to the pool and drank deeply. He would later tell me, "That was the stupidest decision I've ever made."

Guinea worm is a parasite which lives in contaminated waters in Africa. The larvae live in the water flea. When a human ingests the tiny flea in his drinking water, he unknowingly ingests the larvae as well. At least 16,000 villages in eighteen countries in Africa are plagued by guinea worm. According to the Carter Center, over 200,000 people suffer from the parasite annually. Some remote villages have seen a fifty percent infection rate. Although death is rare with guinea worm, its effects are incredibly painful and debilitating. As little Francois drank the dirty water, he had no idea that life would soon turn into a living nightmare.

At first something like pimples appeared on his legs. Eventually they became swollen and painful and began to look like boils. For the little ten-year-old, the pain was excruciating. He would cry when his father touched the sensitive areas. The worm was visible just below the skin in a zigzag pattern up his leg for over two feet in length.

An old village neighbor advised bursting the abscesses with a sterile instrument. Francois' eyes about popped out when his father came into the house holding a red hot screw in some tongs. While his brothers held him down, Francois screamed as his father punctured the abscesses formed by the worm. After composing himself, he looked in amazement as the end of the worm became visible. It actually wiggled within the wound.

At this point one might be tempted to simply pull out the worm. This would kill the worm causing the two- to three-foot-long parasite to decompose inside the body. The victim would probably die of blood poisoning.

The only way to deal with this medical horror is to simply allow the worm to wiggle out on his own. The exposed worm is then rolled up on a matchstick as it emerges. The process is painful and lasts up to a month.

Francois pulled out ten worms over the next five months. So painful were the worms that he could not walk during that time. His legs atrophied somewhat, and he lay in bed for weeks. Indeed, he walks with a limp to this day. After six months of being bedridden, he had to learn all over again how to walk and run. Eventually, he recovered from the illness and went on to complete his education.

Recently, Francois showed me the scars from over thirty years ago. As an agricultural engineer in Abidjan, Francois has gone on to become a strong disciple as well as a successful business-man. He will never forget, however, the damage that one stupid decision brought to his life. He knows that in Africa, the careless suffer and quite often do not survive at all.

✟

It always amazes me how one small act can change your entire life. A simple decision can make all the difference. Often we do not understand the weight of our actions at the time. As the weeks and months unfold, however, we go on to suffer or enjoy the consequences. This is why consistent righteousness is so crucial in life. We must do what is right because it is right. It may be that we will not see the wisdom of those decisions until later. On the other hand, a decision to do wrong may not seem so bad at the time, but later on our regret will be deep.

A Christian in Mozambique was waiting for a minibus to take him back to South Africa recently. When the bus came, it was hopelessly crowded with twenty-five people. The attendant prodded him to crowd in, hang on and pay up. Instead, the brother thought the situation to be dangerous and opted to wait for the next bus. He stood on the sidewalk for a while, knowing he would be delayed till the next bus left. Later on, as he headed home in another bus, he stared in shock at the sight before him. There was the first bus, crashed and overturned in a ditch by the road. Twenty-three passengers had died. Arms and legs literally littered the roadway. One good decision had saved his life.

King David unknowingly made an incredibly important and nearly disastrous decision that is described in 2 Samuel 11:1:

> In the spring, at the time when kings go off to war, David sent Joab out with the king's men and the whole Israelite army. They destroyed the Ammonites and besieged Rabbah. But David remained in Jerusalem.

David decided not to accompany his army into battle. Instead, he sent Joab out with his men to fight for Israel. David, meanwhile, stayed in the palace.

It was a bad decision. Leaders should not lead from the back. True leaders lead at the front. So often one bad decision leads to another, and so it was with David:

> One evening David got up from his bed and walked around on the roof of the palace. From the roof he saw a woman bathing. The woman was very beautiful, and David sent someone to find out about her. The man said, "Isn't this Bathsheba, the daughter of Eliam and the wife of Uriah the Hittite?" Then David sent messengers to get her. She came to him, and he slept with her. (She had purified herself from her uncleanness.) Then she went back home. The woman conceived and sent word to David, saying, "I am pregnant" (2 Samuel 11:2-5).

He saw a woman bathing. He should have looked away, but instead he looked anyway. What followed was adultery, drunkenness, lying, betrayal, murder and cover-up.

My point here is that the course of David's life was forever changed by a couple of bad choices. Some seemingly enjoyable and insignificant iniquity turned into a disaster. David did not know it at the time, but he was standing at a fork in the road of his life. He did not realize it that night, as he stared at the bathing Bathsheba, but the impact of his sin would almost destroy him. Certainly his family and kingdom would be ripped apart.

We are in the same situation today. It's the seemingly little decisions in life that can destroy us. As a Christian, one often stands at a fork in the road to heaven without even realizing it. Small temptations come before us, demanding a decision. It's important that we be warned in advance of the consequences. Let us not be like Francois, who unknowingly drank the contaminated water. Let us not imitate David, who greatly damaged his influence in the final years of his life.

Allow me to list examples of four seemingly small temptations that Satan will try to use to drag us out of the light. Most of us will likely face some of these in the next eighteen months. Each of these may not seem significant at the time. Later on, however, you will see that each one has the power to derail your spiritual life.

*Temptation #1: An awesome job offer far from a church of disciples.*

Although we are spreading out as a church into more and more cities, one tactic used by Satan is to isolate you from other disciples. At a Pentagon briefing during the Gulf War, Colin Powell described his attack plan against the Iraqi army. "First we're going to cut it off; then we're going to kill it." This is exactly how disciples get spiritually sick today. First you cut yourself off. Then Satan moves in for the kill.

Let's be honest. Would someone wanting to fashion a life in theater move to Culpepper, Virginia? As beautiful a town as

Culpepper is, no one believes it to be a theater hub. Rather, you would get as close to Broadway or London as possible. And do you think Tom Cruise would be a household name if he had moved to Hollywood, Missouri, instead of Hollywood, California? Of course not. Obviously, it helped him to be at the center of all the action in the film industry. In the same way, you and I need the encouragement, fellowship, friendship, love and support which comes from being near other strong Christians. Isolation only makes it tougher.

Don't think you are going to do well spiritually if you insist on doing the exact opposite of what the Bible commands. You and I both need fellowship and friendship. Turn down the lucrative offers in remote places. We all need spiritual friendships to finish the race. My conviction is that no matter how much they are willing to pay you to work far from other Christians, it is simply not worth it. Those who try to live the Christian life all alone simply fade away spiritually. If there is no church there and you are not going on a mission team there, then why risk it? Rather, heed the Hebrews warning in Hebrews 10:24-25.

> *And let us consider how we may spur one another on toward love and good deeds. Let us not give up meeting together, as some are in the habit of doing, but let us encourage one another— and all the more as you see the Day approaching.*

You need the church services as well as the friendships, and so do I. Don't let Satan buy you out of the kingdom with some job offer in some faraway place.

*Temptation #2: "We'll pay you double to work on Sundays."*
Satan does not have to move you to another city to remove you from the fellowship. Sometimes he finds a pushover who will miss services while still living near the church! My convictions here are just as strong as for #1 above. Whatever they are willing to pay you for work on Sundays, it simply is not worth it. When you miss services, you miss out on the encouragement gleaned from the singing, sermons, classes and conversations. More than this, you miss out on the joy that comes from bringing visitors, giving encouragement and ministering to the needs of others, because we do not go to church only to receive. We go to give as well. Those who decide to miss the assemblies weaken quickly.

The Bible teaches us to seek first the kingdom of God (Matthew 6:33). If you seek his kingdom second or third behind TV shows, career aspirations or Sunday Little League, you certainly will not help your friends or family to be saved. They will see your wimpy commitment. They will see your hypocrisy. Only too late will you realize that you traded away your own spiritual health and the salvation of your loved ones for a few measly bucks earned by capitulating to your boss' demands or for the sake of your child's advancement in the Little League circuit. The Christian who decides to miss the occasional service is much like Francois drinking the contaminated water. Spiritual disaster awaits him.

*Temptation #3: "I'm too busy to pray and read my Bible."*

This is another surefire recipe for falling away. Each day you make the seemingly small decision of whether you will spend time building your relationship with God by studying the Bible and praying to him. It is a crucial decision for every Christian. Just as an overweight person cannot ask which french fry made him fat, the weak Christian cannot ask which missed quiet time made him weak. It is a cumulative process. It takes time.

Eventually, however, the Christian who neglects the Scriptures and prayer usually walks away from his faith. It's just that simple.

I will not tell you some legalistic time requirement for daily devotions to God. As a young Christian I felt like I was standing on the top of Mount Sinai after a thirty-minute prayer time. Today, nearly twenty years later, I feel that thirty minutes of prayer is rather rushed. However, only you know the quality of your prayer and Bible study. I am calling you to deepen both. Quality is crucial. Of course, if you are not reading or praying much at all these days, my experience tells me you will not be a disciple for much longer. If Jesus saw his need to pray and know the Scriptures, imagine how great our need is. Look at Jeremiah's attitude:

> *When your words came I ate them;*
> *    they were my joy and my heart's delight,*
> *for I bear your name,*
> *    O Lord God Almighty  (Jeremiah 15:16).*

Or notice Peter's reverence for God's word:

> *Like newborn babies, crave pure spiritual milk, so that by*
> *it you may grow up in your salvation (1 Peter 2:2).*

Your time with God, your prayer and Bible study, is your umbilical cord to God. It's a lifeline of spiritual nourishment flowing into your soul. If you cut it off, you will simply shrivel up and die spiritually. It is that simple.

*Temptation #4: Romance with a non-Christian.*

There is no doubt about it. I meet lots of people who do not believe in Jesus yet at the same time are attractive, witty and intelligent. Christians are not the only nice people on the planet! But getting involved romantically with a non-Christian is an unwise decision. The Bible is very straightforward about this. The wisest man to ever live, Solomon, fell because of his involvement with unbelieving women. The strongest man who ever lived, Samson, fell because of his involvement with unbelieving women. The Bible commands us not to yoke ourselves into commitments with non-Christians (and that would certainly include romantic ones) for very good reason. It is a yoke that will probably ruin you.

> *Do not be yoked together with unbelievers. For what do righteousness and wickedness have in common? Or what fellowship can light have with darkness? What harmony is there between Christ and Belial? What does a believer have in common with an unbeliever? What agreement is there between the temple of God and idols? For we are the temple of the living God. As God has said: "I will live with them and walk among them, and I will be their God, and they will be my people."*
>
> *"Therefore come out from them*
>     *and be separate,*
>                     *says the Lord.*
> *Touch no unclean thing*
>     *and I will receive you."*
> *"I will be a Father to you,*
>     *and you will be my sons and daughters,*
>                     *says the Lord Almighty"*
>                     *(2 Corinthians 6:14-18).*

When I started studying the Bible, I was dating a very intelligent and attractive woman. Although she had a very nice personality, when I decided to follow Jesus, she made it clear she was not interested. I broke it off fairly quickly.

Have I ever regretted my decision? No way. I thank God that he later led me to marry Anne-Brigitte. Her faith, conviction and determination to imitate Jesus have encouraged me countless times over the years. I very likely would not be a Christian today were it not for her help and friendship.

I know that sometimes Christians who are single can feel lonely and rejected. They miss the security of romance that they had in the world. They wonder how long it will be before they find Mr. or Miss Right in the kingdom. Satan is very adept at using this situation. He will try to encourage romance with a non-Christian as much as possible. It usually begins slowly. An invitation to lunch or coffee. A lift home. A harmless encounter. Pretty soon romance is taking root, and you are having to decide between staying with Mr./Miss Right or following Jesus. It is obviously better to avoid the whole situation entirely. Romance with a nonbeliever tends to make you one as well. The worm of faithlessness gets into your life and winds its way through more and more of your thinking.

If you are already married to a nonbeliever, let Peter's words encourage you:

*Wives, in the same way be submissive to your husbands so that, if any of them do not believe the word, they may be won over without words by the behavior of their wives, when they see the purity and reverence of your lives (1 Peter 3:1-2).*

Although written to women, the principle is true for men, as well. The purity and reverence of your life is the major element in winning over your spouse. So don't give up hope. Keep on praying. (However, all of those who have not yet married and have a choice in the matter should realize what a big decision whom we date will turn out to be.)

It's the seemingly little decisions in life that often determine our fate. Our Bible study and prayer, the city we live in, our schedule and our choice of whom we will date, all have far-reaching and eternal ramifications. God honors you with the freedom to decide for yourself through prayer, getting advice and sober reflection, but he promises you that the best course is to always seek first his kingdom. We must understand this point. These are crucial decisions.

So often it's the seemingly small decisions that change the course of your life and steer you toward new horizons. Many times we do not even recognize the import of the decision at the time. For that reason, we must always strive to be righteous— even when the matter seems inconsequential or innocuous. Just as a young driver typically does not see the value of obeying the speed limit, his obedience is blessed all the same. Later on, after having driven past a dozen or more fatal accidents on the highway, he realizes the wisdom of the decision to drive carefully.

✠

In the late 1800s, a British member of Parliament was en route to Scotland from London in order to give a speech. His carriage, however, became stuck in mud along a country road. Getting out to assess the situation, the lawmaker stared at the mess in front of him. There was nothing he could do.

About this time a young lad appeared from a nearby field with a team of horses ready to help. Within a few moments the carriage was safe, and he was ready to resume his journey.

"How can I repay you?" asked the parliamentarian.

"I cannot accept payment for simply being a good neighbor," replied the lad.

Impressed, the old man persisted, "What do you want to be when you grow up?"

The boy glanced downward for a moment. "I'd like to study medicine," he replied, "but obviously there is no way my family can ever afford the school fees."

"Then I shall help you do it," declared the old gentleman. And the lawyer kept his word.

Almost fifty years later, during World War II, with the fate of Britain hanging in the balance, another famous British statesman was lying ill in London. Winston Churchill had contracted pneumonia and was close to death in an English hospital while Hitler's forces were amassing across the English Channel.

Churchill managed to recover, thanks to an injection of a new drug called "penicillin." Recently discovered by Alexander

Fleming, the drug saved England's leader at a crucial time in her history.

Alexander Fleming, the 1945 cowinner of the Nobel Prize for medicine and physiology, was the boy who had pulled out the lawmaker's carriage from the mud. And the rich lawmaker who paid for his education was Sir Randolph Churchill, the father of Winston Churchill.

There was no possible way that the boy could have known that because of his act of kindness to the old man, his medical education would be paid for. And there was no possible way that the politician could have known that by paying for the boy's education, he was actually saving the life of his son. And perhaps his nation as well.

Both men did the right thing simply because it was right. Without realizing it, the small and seemingly insignificant decisions which they made not only changed the course of their lives, but of their nation as well.

In any situation, do the right thing. Make the right choice. You may not see the consequences of it today. You may not know the results for a decade. But in doing the right thing, in taking the narrow road, you will be blessed forever.

# EPILOGUE

In 1989 I took the short flight from Abidjan to Liberia to meet a captain in the president's bodyguard. He was eager to study the Bible and become a disciple. A civil war was raging in the countryside, and although the capital was a safe distance from the fighting, people were worried and tense.

I was staying in a shoddy hotel room in the downtown. We were using the day to read the Bible together, but at times when his duties called the captain away, I would sit idly in my room. My mind, however, was not in Liberia. Rather, it was focused on an operating theater thousands of miles away in the states. My father was undergoing emergency heart surgery that day in Virginia. I waited until I thought the operation would be over, then I placed the call.

I can't tell you how delighted I was to learn that he had come through the operation with flying colors. He was fine, and to this day he insists that he feels even better than he did before his surgery. I thank God daily that he gave my father a brand new heart. To this day I get a lump in my throat when I see my boys sitting on his lap. Praise God for modern medicine. Praise God for second chances.

I don't know the condition of your heart today as you read these words. We live in a spiritual jungle, and the dangers to our health are real and formidable. Some of you may be weak, others strong. The most important point I can make is that God is still in the business of renewing our hearts today. God is the God of hope, of renewal and of second chances. He wants to see you happy and victorious.

The challenges I've described in this book are real and are dangerous. Sin stalks you and desires to infect your faith in God. Jesus, however, is still the Great Physician. If you are weak, he can help you to recover. If you are strong, he can give you guidance in preventing spiritual illness. Jesus stands by our side to help us as we walk through the jungles of the shadow of death.

Christianity is not easy. When you decided to follow Jesus, you chose the more difficult path. Doing wrong has always been easy, while standing up and doing the right thing calls for courage, determination and discipline. At times we feel tired. Occasionally we feel weak. It's at times like that when we must rush back to the Master's side. The Great Physician is ready to renew our hearts completely.

Of course, don't forget that the best medicine is preventative medicine. Your grandmother was right when she told you that an ounce of prevention is worth a pound of cure. Just as you exercise your heart, you must exercise your faith. Getting out there and *living* the Christian life is the best prescription a disciple can receive. Whether it is sharing your faith, loving your enemy, inviting your neighbors to church, helping the poor or having a great prayer with a friend, practicing your faith will always leave you flushed with joy and renewed in spirit.

I suppose it's true that if my dad had exercised a little more and eaten more healthful foods, he might not ever have needed the operation. I believe that's the best antidote to spiritual weakness: Stay spiritually fit by constantly practicing your faith. That in itself will go a long way in keeping the spiritual Ebolas, Guinea worms and all the other diseases far from your heart forever.

Once I was sitting in a restaurant with Steve Johnson in New York. I shared with him how I hadn't been sharing my faith much lately, and I needed to change. I expected a deep conversation about how I felt, what I was going through, and a long talk about my heart. Instead he simply said, "Why don't you invite the waitress?"

It was so simple, but so true. Action is far more refreshing than analysis. Getting out and practicing our faith is far more exciting than lying back on the couch and going through your life history and trying to understand why you are not naturally evangelistic.

So I invited the waitress, and I kept on inviting people. Within the next seven months, I helped fifteen people to be baptized into Christ. I was totally refreshed, and a little wiser as well. Jesus calls for action. It doesn't have to be complicated or a long, drawn-out process. You can begin right now. Sure, I've talked a lot about being open and having honest conversations about where you are in your life. Yes, go ahead and have those talks. But don't go on and on about it. Action is crucial to your spiritual health.

So as you put down this book, go ahead and take a look around. Who needs to be invited to church? Where are the poor who need to be cared for? Who needs a helping hand? I bet you'll find that the more you reach out and offer a helping hand today to others, the more motivated you'll be to do it in the future.

That's the key to spiritual health. The more you focus on the spiritual health of others, the more healthy you become as well.

Sin is very real. It is as real as the Ebola virus, cholera, cancer, meningitis, tetanus, and the Guinea worm. But while even disciples fall victim to some of these dread diseases, sin need never win a final victory in our lives. Through the power of Christ and the fellowship of his people, righteousness can rule, and we can know the abundant life.

# BIBLIOGRAPHY

Destexhe, Alain. *Rwanda and Genocide in the Twentieth Century.* New York, New York: University Press, 1994.

Farrar, Steve. *Finishing Strong.* Sisters, Oregon: Multnomah Books, 1995.

Harries, A.D., M.D., Harries, J.R., M.D. and Cook, G.C., M.D. *100 Clinical Problems in Tropical Medicine.* London: Balliere Tindall, 1987.

Newton, Alex. *Central Africa: A Travel Survival Kit.* Hawthorn, Australia: Lonely Planet, 1994.

Reeves, Thomas C. *The Empty Church.* New York, New York: Free Press, 1996.

Robinson Family Health. *The Family Encyclopedia of Medicine and Health.* London: Robinson Publishing, 1996.

Smith, Tony, M.D., Ed. *The Macmillan Guide to Family Health.* London: Macmillan, 1992.

Vassall-Adams, Guy. *Rwanda: An Agenda for International Action.* Oxford: Oxfam Publications, 1994.

# Who Are We?

Discipleship Publications International (DPI) began publishing in 1993. We are a non-profit Christian publisher committed to publishing and distributing materials that honor God, lift up Jesus Christ and show how his message practically applies to all areas of life. We have a deep conviction that no one changes life like Jesus and that the implementation of his teaching will revolutionize any life, any marriage, any family and any singles household.

Since our beginning we have published more than 100 titles; plus we have produced a number of important, spiritual audio products. More than one million volumes have been printed, and our works have been translated into more than a dozen languages—international is not just a part of our name! Our books are shipped monthly to every inhabited continent.

To see a more detailed description of our works, find us on the World Wide Web at **www.dpibooks.org**. You can order books by calling 1-888-DPI-BOOK 24 hours a day.

We appreciate the hundreds of comments we have received from readers. We would love to hear from you. Here are other ways to get in touch:

**Mail:** DPI, 2 Sterling Road, Billerica, MA 01862-2595
**E-mail:** dpibooks@icoc.org

# Find Us on the World Wide Web

www.dpibooks.org